Coding for Beginners Using HTML, CSS & JavaScript

Textbook

8

Sangita Chadha

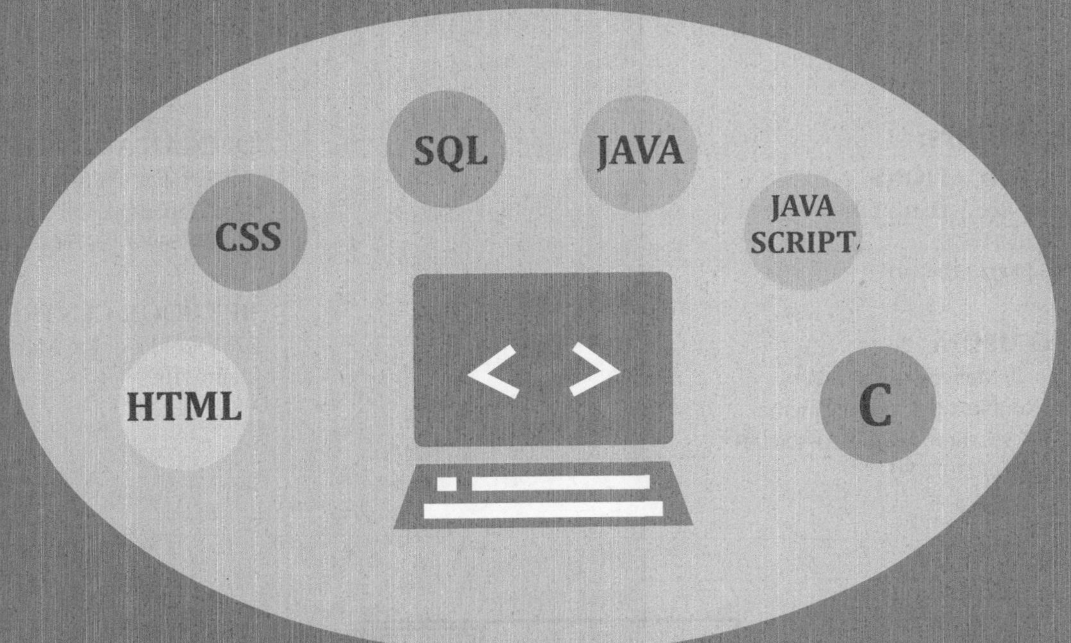

www.bpbonline.com

FIRST EDITION 2022
REPRINT 2026

ISBN: 978-93-5551-232-1

LIMITS OF LIABILITY AND DISCLAIMER OF WARRANTY

The information contained in this book is true to correct and the best of author's and publisher's knowledge. The author has made every effort to ensure the accuracy of these publications, but publisher cannot be held responsible for any loss or damage arising from any information in this book.

All trademarks referred to in the book are acknowledged as properties of their respective owners but BPB Publications cannot guarantee the accuracy of this information.

CBSE is in no way connected with this book. This Book is written solely for the benefit and guidance of students appearing of CBSE Examination.

Distributors:

BPB PUBLICATIONS
20, Ansari Road, Darya Ganj
New Delhi-110002
Ph: 23254990/23254991

MICRO MEDIA
Shop No. 5, Mahendra Chambers,
150 DN Rd. Next to Capital Cinema,
V.T. (C.S.T.) Station, MUMBAI-400 001
Ph: 22078296/22078297

DECCAN AGENCIES
4-3-329, Bank Street,
Hyderabad-500195
Ph: 24756967/24756400

BPB BOOK CENTRE
376 Old Lajpat Rai Market,
Delhi-110006
Ph: 23861747

To View Complete BPB Publications Catalogue Scan the QR Code:

Published by Manish Jain for BPB Publications, 20 Ansari Road, Darya Ganj, New Delhi-110002 and Printed by him at Manipal Technologies Limited, Manipal

www.bpbonline.com

Dedicated to

My children and students

About the Authors

Sangita Chadha has been working as Head of Computer Department in Ambience Public School, Safdarjung Enclave, New Delhi from last 14 years. She has over twenty years of experience in the field of education; teaching Computer Science, Informatics Practices and Multimedia & Web Technology to grades XI and XII; and has been multifold responsibilities at her school (Result In-charge, ERP, Website, Almanac, Magazine). She is a passionate learner and committed educator consistently working to make learning enjoyable for the learners.Her foremost classroom pedagogy is centered around project-based learning. She has conducted ICT and Net safety workshops for all stakeholders. She has been part of the curriculum development team for classes IX and X Information and Communication Technology, NCERT. She has co-authored class IX and X ICT for NCERT. She also co-authored Class XII Informatics Practices and Computer Science, NCERT. She has conducted Teacher Training workshops for SCERT Teachers.

Acknowledgements

I would like to acknowledge the contributions of all the educators, data scientists, scientists, professionals from various fields for their valuable suggestions in developing the content for this book.

I would like to express my gratitude to everyone at BPB Publications for giving us this opportunity to write the book. I am thankful to all the resource persons at BPB Publications for editing, technical reviewing and language editing the book. I would like to thank our technical reviewer, Mrs. Rekha Verma for her thoughtful insights while refining the manuscript of this book.

I am thankful to my family for being supportive in numerous ways and for giving their unconditional love and support at all times.

Lastly, but not the least, I would like to thank God for bearing us with courage and humility to be able to write this book for our students.

— Sangita Chadha

Preface

The primary objective in the development of this book series is to create a fun learning and project-based approach to learn to code. With the help of this, the student will be able to understand, identify and apply the fundamentals of a programming language. It also builds problem-solving skills.

Book will bring an innovative approach among students by Project-based learning which fosters creativity, critical thinking, and innovative ideas that enable a deeper understanding of concepts which leads to longer retention.

The students will start with the approach of looking at the application first and then follow the steps to build an application.

Contents

Installation Guide

Visual Studio Code can be used as an excellent editor for many languages with the help of extensions. It is simple, easy, fun, small in size, and productive. The available extensions make it an excellent editor and are operating system independent.

Students are required to go through the following links to download and install Visual Studio Code.

Follow the instructions while using the links given below as per your operating system to install Visual Studio Code:

- **Visual Studio Code on Linux:**

  https://code.visualstudio.com/docs/setup/linux

- **Visual Studio Code on macOS:**

  https://code.visualstudio.com/docs/setup/mac

- **Visual Studio Code on Windows:**

  https://code.visualstudio.com/docs/setup/windows

- **Open in Browser from Extensions:**

  Once installed the Visual Studio Code, click on the extension and search for Open in Browser and install it.

- **Check out the following links to know more about the Visual Studio code:**

  https://code.visualstudio.com/docs

  https://code.visualstudio.com/docs/getstarted/tips-and-tricks

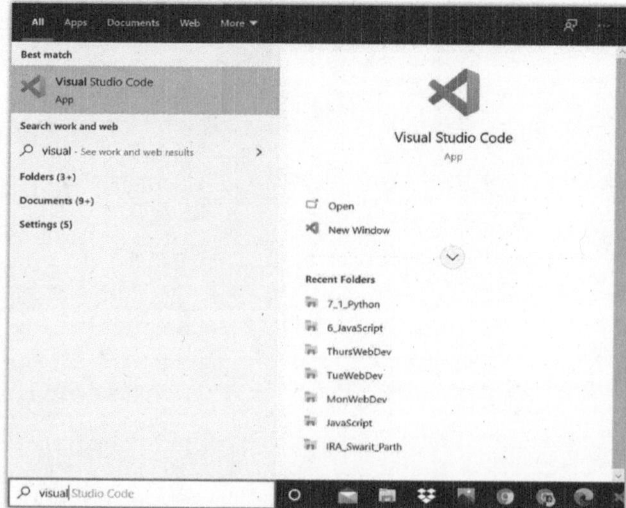

Figure 1: *Opening of Visual Studio Code*

Steps to use Visual Studio Code:

- Open Visual Studio Code: Click on the Windows key and type in Visual Studio Code. Click on Visual Studio Code to open the application.
- The Visual Studio Code application looks like as shown in figure 2.

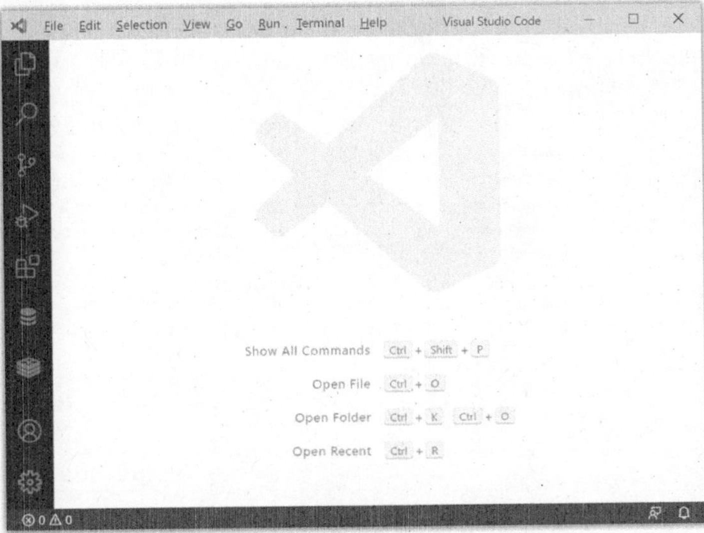

***Figure 2:** Visual Studio Code window*

- Now, let us open the folder (i.e. the work area) to place all the python files in that folder. Click on File Open Folder as shown in figure 3 and then choose the folder to work with.

  For first-time users, a new folder needs to be created.

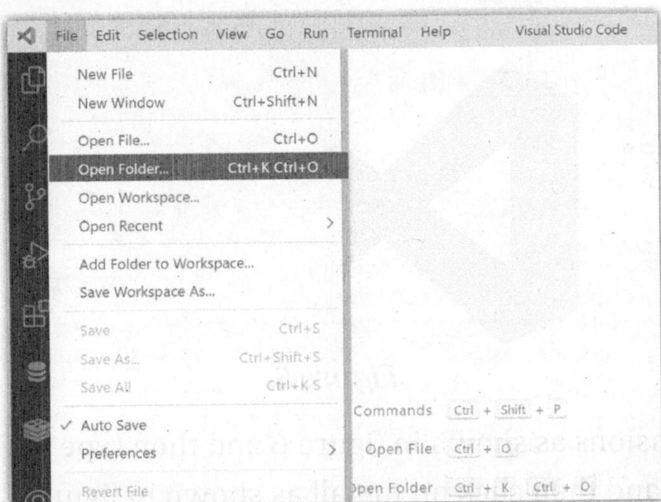

***Figure 3 (a):** Open Folder*

Choose the path, click on New Folder, and give a name to the folder as shown in figure 4 (For first-time users). Then click on the folder name to choose it and click on Select Folder as shown in figure 5, it will open the work area for your python files in Visual Studio Code.

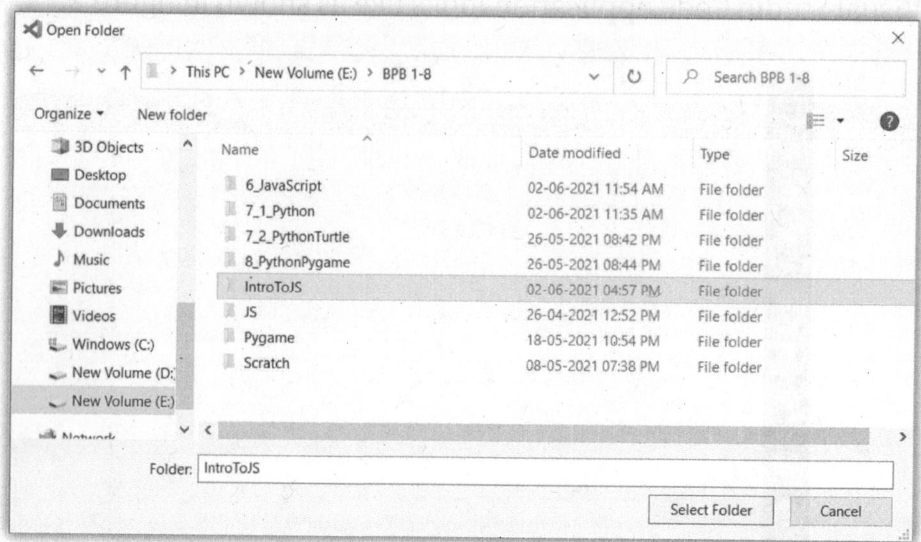

Figure 4

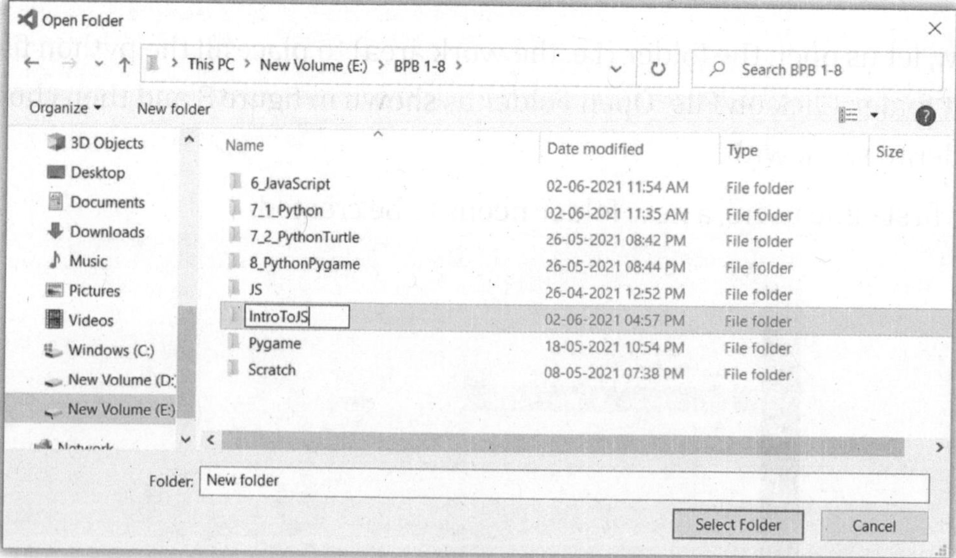

Figure 5

Click on the Extensions as shown in figure 6 and then type in Open in Browser in the search bar and then click on Install as shown in figure 7.

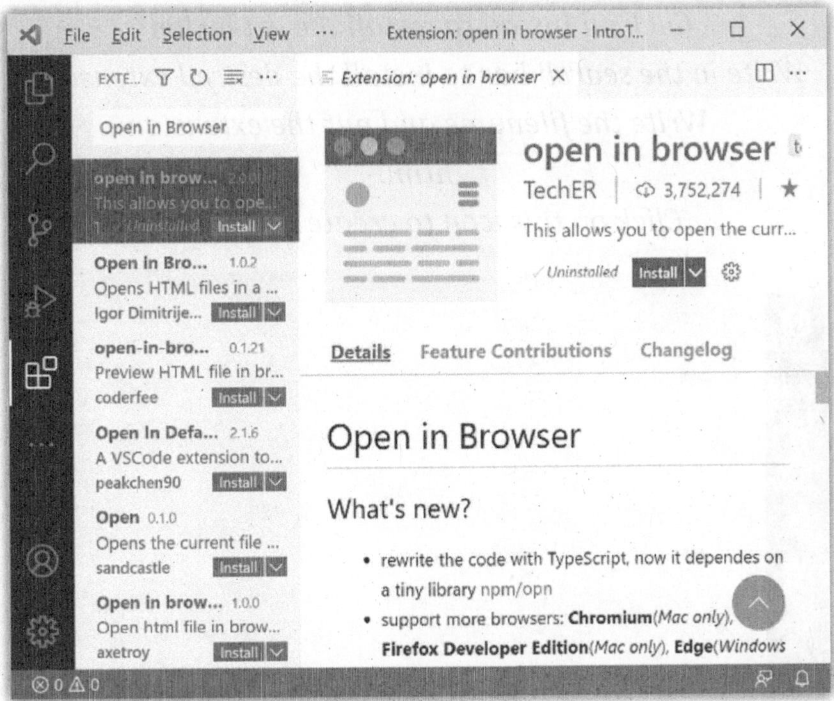

Figure 6

Click on this icon to open extensions to be installed.

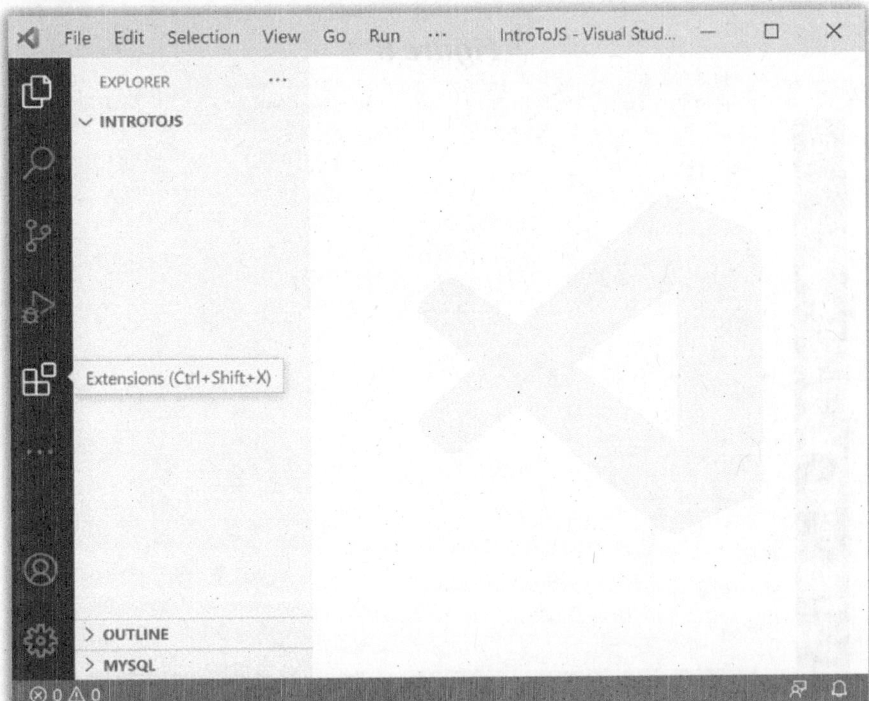

Figure 7

Click on Install to install the extension.

Write in the search bar to install the desired extension.

Write the filename and put the extension .html.

Click on this icon to create a new file.

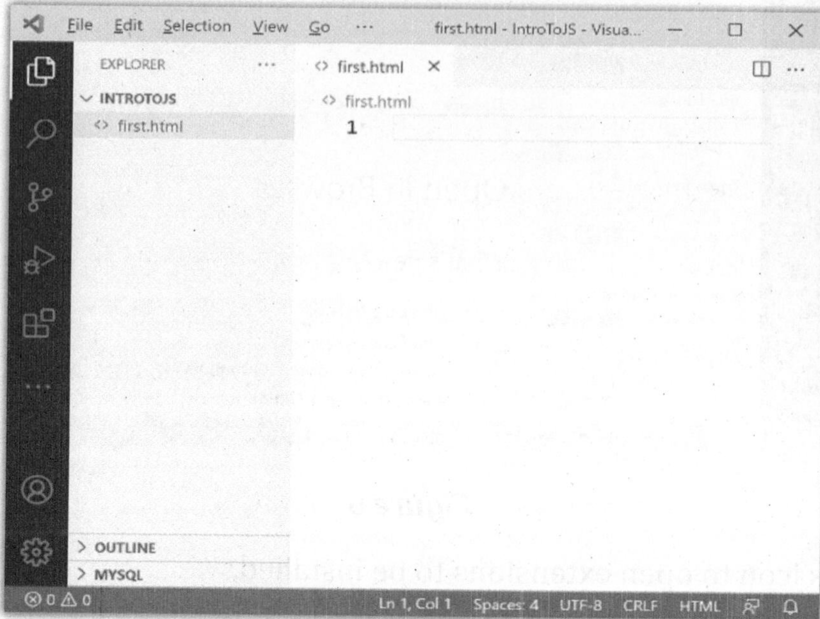

Figure 8

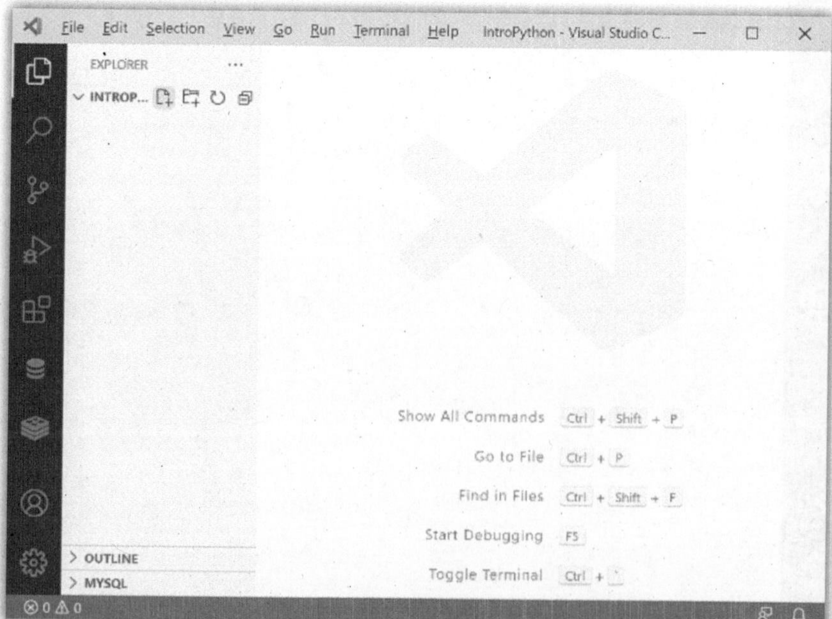

Figure 8

Code Editor window.

Right-click on anywhere in the code editor window and choose Open in Default Browser.

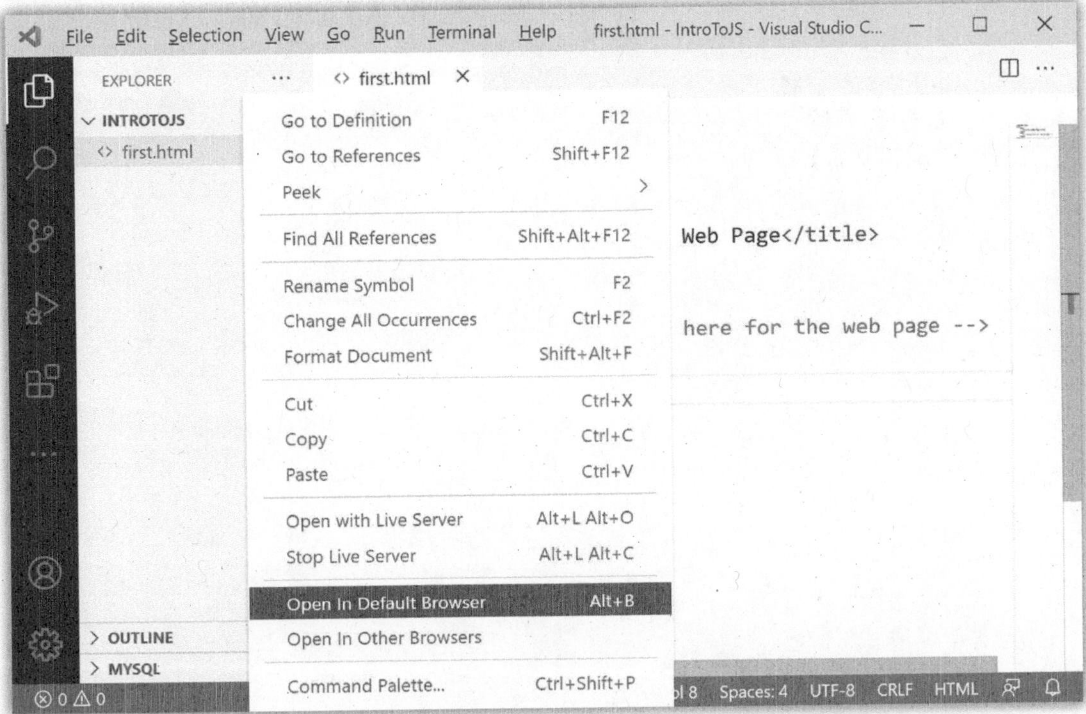

Figure 10: *Visual Studio Code window*

Introduction to HTML, CSS and JavaScript

Structure

In this chapter, you will learn and practice the following concepts:

- HTML document structure
- Internal style sheet
- DOM inner HTML property
- Use of alert()

Learning Objective

At the end of this chapter, you will be able to:

- Do simple mathematical problems using input, output, and arithmetic operators
- Project –A simple calculator

Introduction to HTML

- HTML is Hyper Text Markup Language.
- It is a language for creating web pages.
- HTML is used to give the structure of the web page.
- The web page can include text, images, videos, etc.
- The HTML uses predefined tags which are interpreted by the browser.
- The browser is an application that helps to open web pages.

Structure of HTML Document

The HTML element defines the root element of the HTML web page.

The HTML tag is written within <> and has different properties.

The HTML document contains two parts:

- **HEAD:** It contains meta-information about the HTML web page.
- **BODY:** It contains the information which will be displayed on the web page.

Info bot

The HTML element is defined by a start tag followed by some content and an end tag.

Activity 1.1

Create the HTML web page as shown in figure 1.1(a)

In this activity, we will be using the following:

- **HTML:** To define the content for the web pages.
- **CSS:** To specify the layout of web pages.
- **JavaScript:** To program the behaviour of web pages.

Title of the webpage

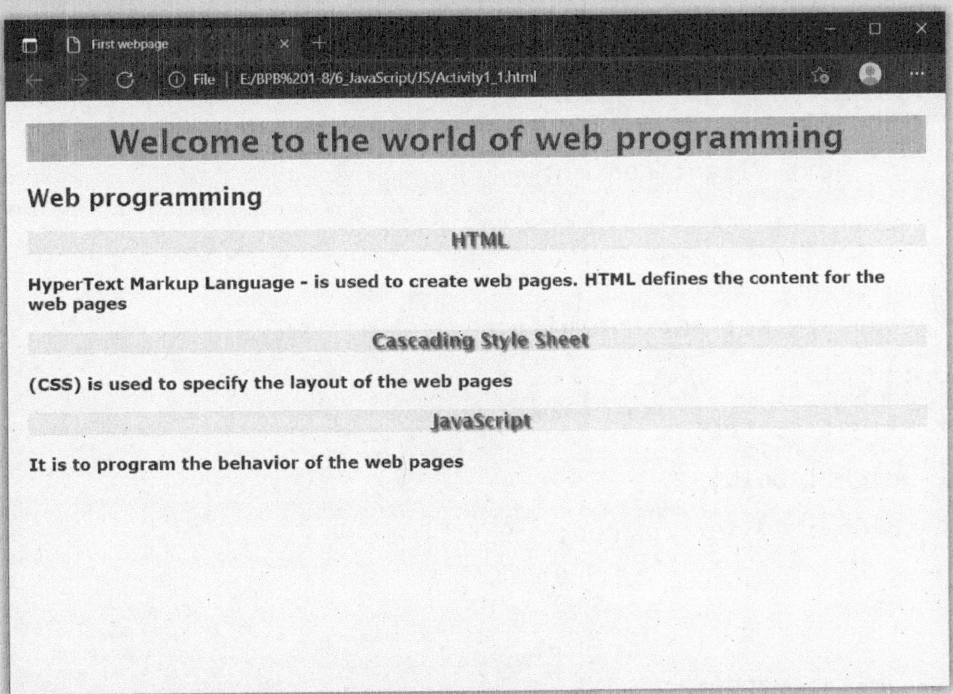

Body of the webpage

Figure 1.1(a): Output window for Activity 1.1

Info bot

The internal style sheet is written within <style></style> tags in the head section of the HTML document to change the appearance of the HTML tags.

Code for Activity 1.1

```
<!DOCTYPE html>
<html>
  <head><title>First webpage</title>
    <style>
      body{
        background-color: azure;
        font-family: lucida sans;
        margin: 20px;
      }
      h1{ background-color: aqua;
        color: blue;
                text-align: center;
        }
      h3{
        background-color: antiquewhite;
        color:purple;
        text-align: center;
        font-weight: bold;
        text-shadow: 2px 2px 2px red;
      }
      p{
        font-family: verdana;
        font-weight: bold;
      }
    </style>
  </head>
  <body>
    <h1>Welcome to the world of web programming</h1>
    <h2>Web programming</h2>
    <h3>HTML</h3>
```

```
    <p>HyperText Markup Language - is used to create web pages. HTML de-
fines the content for the web pages</p>
    <h3>Cascading Style Sheet </h3>
    <p>(CSS) is used to specify the layout of the web pages </p>
    <h3>JavaScript </h3>
    <p>It is to program the behavior of the web pages</p>
  </body>
</html>
```

Explanation:

- There are 6 levels of headings in HTML. H1 is the largest one and H6 being the smallest.
- P tag is used to put the contents in paragraph form.
- Within the style tag, use the HTML tag name to set the properties for that tag as done in this *Activity 1.1*.
- Internal Style Sheet is written within the <style></style> tags of HTML.

Style properties:

- **Background-color:** It is used to select the background color for the HTML tag.
- **Font-family:** To change the style of the font.
- **Margin:** To give space around the object/ element.
- **Color:** To set the foreground color for the tag.
- **Text-align:** To align the text to left/ right/ center/ justify.
- **Font-weight:** To change the font stroke thickness.
- **Text-shadow:** Apply shadow effects to the text.

The <!DOCTYPE html> in the beginning of the webpage defines that it is HTML5 document.

With *Activity 1.1*, we understood by applying the CSS to HTML elements how CSS helps to change the style of the HTML elements. We have seen the **DOM** i.e., **Document Object Model** in our first activity. This clearly shows that the structure of an HTML document consists of two parts – Head and Body.

CSS uses rules that are selectors used to apply properties to the HTML elements. As seen in *Activity 1.1*, all the <p> tags in the webpage are using font Verdana and bold style defined by the CSS.

Now we will try to understand and apply JavaScript through various interactive examples to see how HTML, CSS, and JavaScript are related to one another.

Info bot

JavaScript is the only programming language for which the browser do need not to install any plug-in or extensions.

I would recommend you tweak and play around with the code to learn by seeing the output you get. The more you try and test, the more you will understand the concept.

The Document Object Model of HTML looks as given in the following *figure 1.2*:

***Figure 1.2:** DOM of HTML document*

DOM is used to get, change, add or delete any HTML elements using JavaScript. The very important property/ attribute of any HTML element is the ID which helps JavaScript to work with that HTML element. The **getElementById()** is a method of JavaScript that fetches the HTML element using its ID property. The innerHTML is a property that is used to get/ replace the content of the HTML element using JavaScript.

Create the webpage which will use JavaScript to change the content of an HTML element using DOM innerHTML property.

```
<!DOCTYPE html>
<html>
<head>
    <title>JavaScript-2</title>
</head>
<body>
    <h1>Introduction to JavaScript</h1>
    <h2>Changing the content of HTML element using DOM innerHTML property in JavaScript</h2>
    <p>Here, we have defined the id property for the H2 element and then we are replacing the content of this h2
    element using JavaScript. The element is referenced using getElementById method and replaced using innerHTML
    property. Now when this code is rendered on the browser, you will see the content of H2 element replaced with
    Welcome to the world of JavaScript Programming.</p>
    <h2 id="t1">Changing the text of this H2 element using the DOM innerHTML property with getElementById method. </h2>

    <script>
        document.getElementById("t1").innerHTML = 'Welcome to the world of JavaScript Programming'
    </script>
</body>
</html>
```

Figure 1.3(a): Code window for Activity 1.2

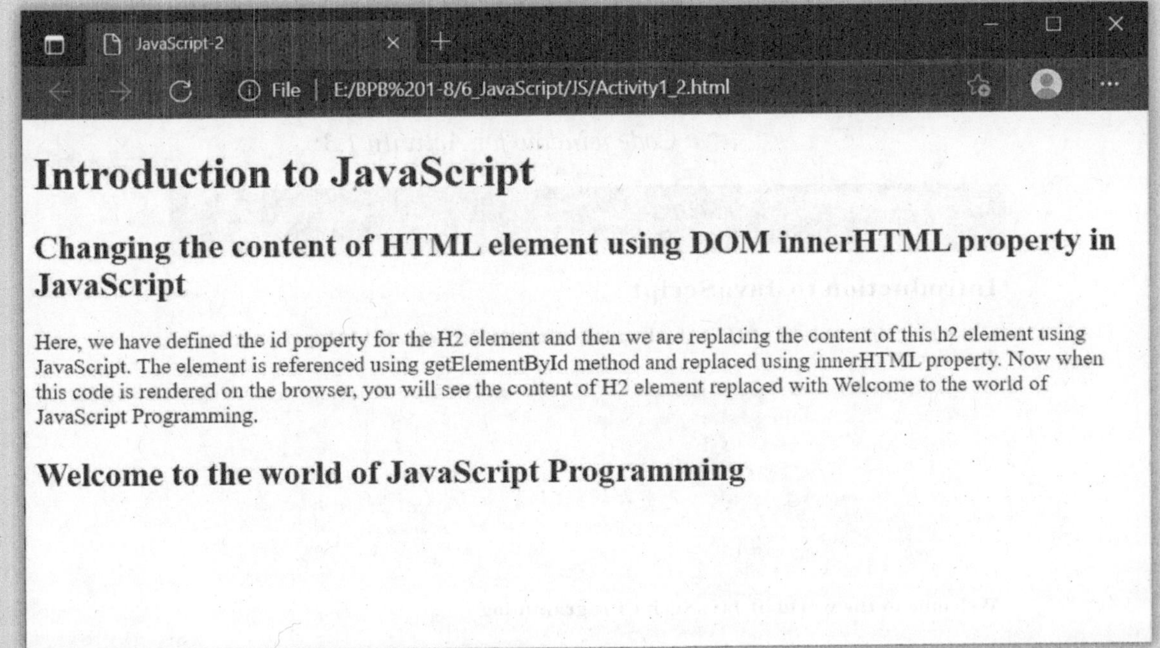

Figure 1.3(b): Output window for Activity 1.2

Activity 1.3

Change the font style to 'Jokerman', the color of the text to 'red', size of content to '20px', background dcolor to 'pink', margin to '20px' and padding to '20px' for the paragraph element using JavaScript in the previous Activity 1.2

To do this activity, save as the above code (figure 1.3(a)) by using another name and make the following changes:

- Add ID property to <P> tag.
- Add the JavaScript code to change the style of the <P> tag as given in the code using <script></script> tags.

```
<!DOCTYPE html>
<html>
<head> <title>JavaScript-3</title>
</head>
<body>
    <h1>Introduction to JavaScript</h1>
    <h2>Changing the content of HTML element using DOM innerHTML property in JavaScript</h2>
    <p id="t2">Here, we have defined the id property for the H2 element and then we are replacing the
    content of this h2 element using JavaScript. The element is referenced using getElementById method
    and replaced using innerHTML property. Now when this code is rendered on the browser, you will see
    the content of H2 element replaced with Welcome to the world of JavaScript Programming.</p>
    <h2 id="t1">Changing the text of this H2 element using the DOM innerHTML property with
    getElementById method. </h2>
    <script>
        document.getElementById("t1").innerHTML = 'Welcome to the world of JavaScript Programming';
        document.getElementById("t2").style.fontFamily='Jokerman';
        document.getElementById("t2").style.fontSize="20px";
        document.getElementById("t2").style.color="red";
        document.getElementById("t2").style.backgroundColor="pink";
        document.getElementById("t2").style.margin="20px";
        document.getElementById("t2").style.padding="20px";
    </script>
</body>
</html>
```

Figure 1.4(a): Code window for Activity 1.3

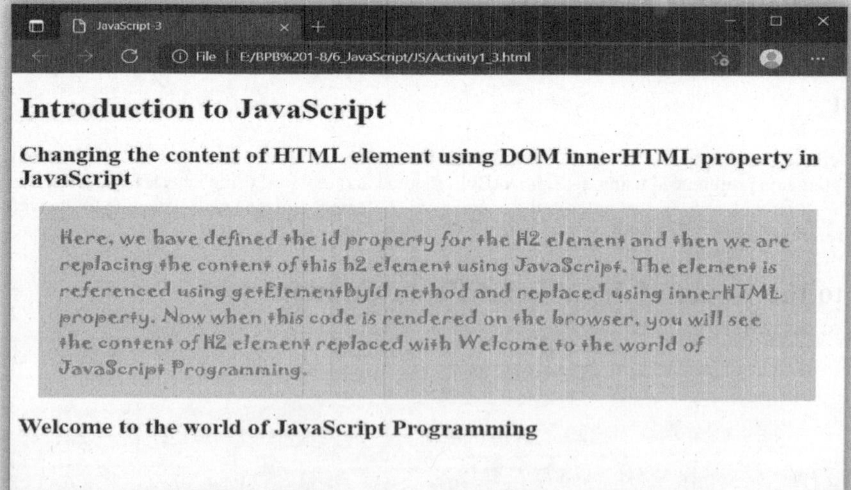

Figure 1.4(b): Output window for Activity 1.3

Activity 1.4

Use the prompt method of JavaScript to take input from the user and store it in a variable and then display the message in another dialog window using the alert method of JavaScript.

```
<!DOCTYPE html>
<html>
<head>
    <title>Event handling</title>
</head>
<body>
    <h1>Introduction to JavaScript prompt and alert method which
    is displayed while loading the webpage</h1>
    <script>
        name=prompt("Enter your name please? ")
        alert("Hello!! "+ name + "\nHave a good day! ")
    </script>
</body>
</html>
```

Figure 1.5(a): Code window for Activity 1.4

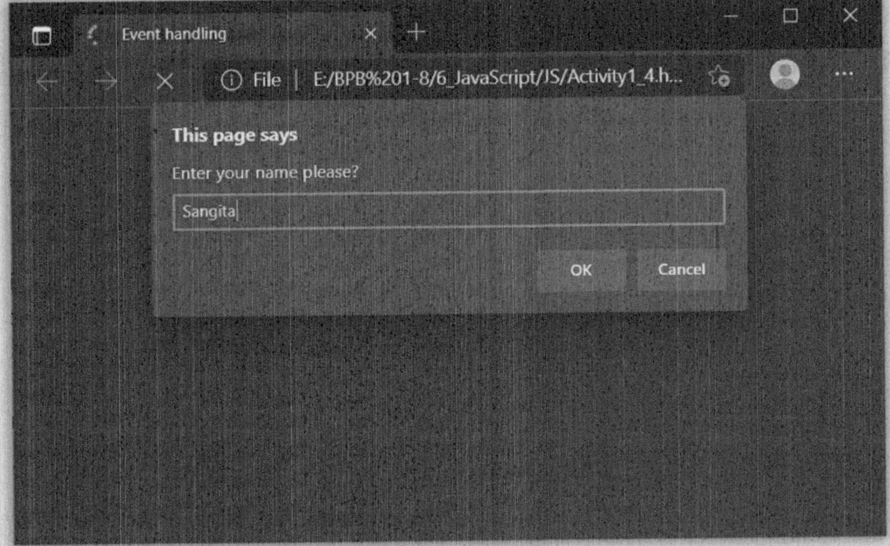

Figure 1.5(b): Output window for Activity 1.4

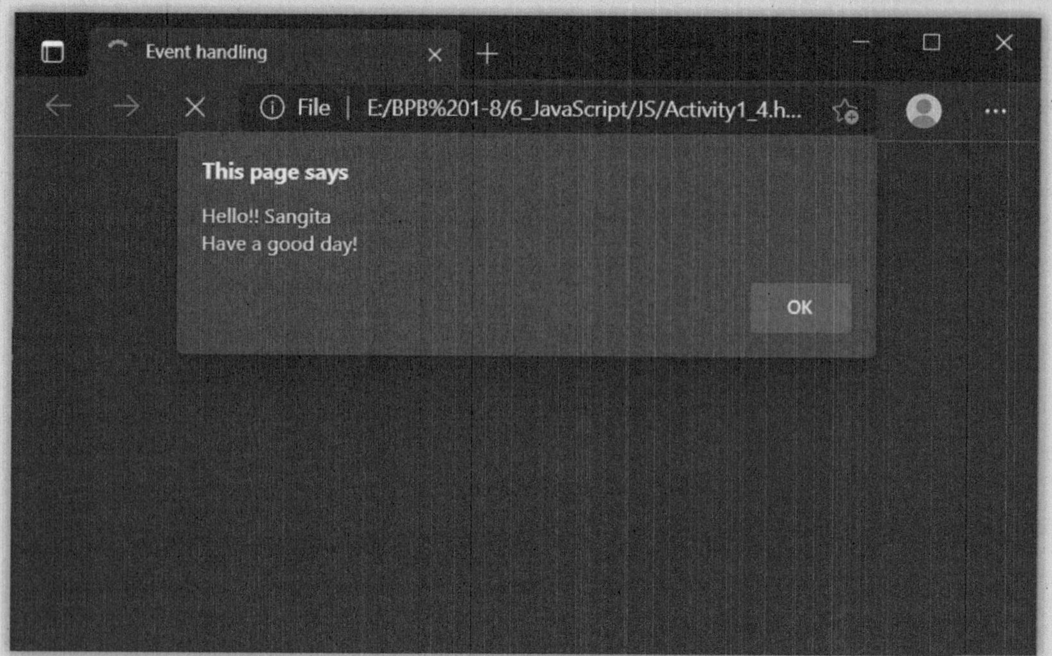

Figure 1.5(c): Output window for Activity 1.4

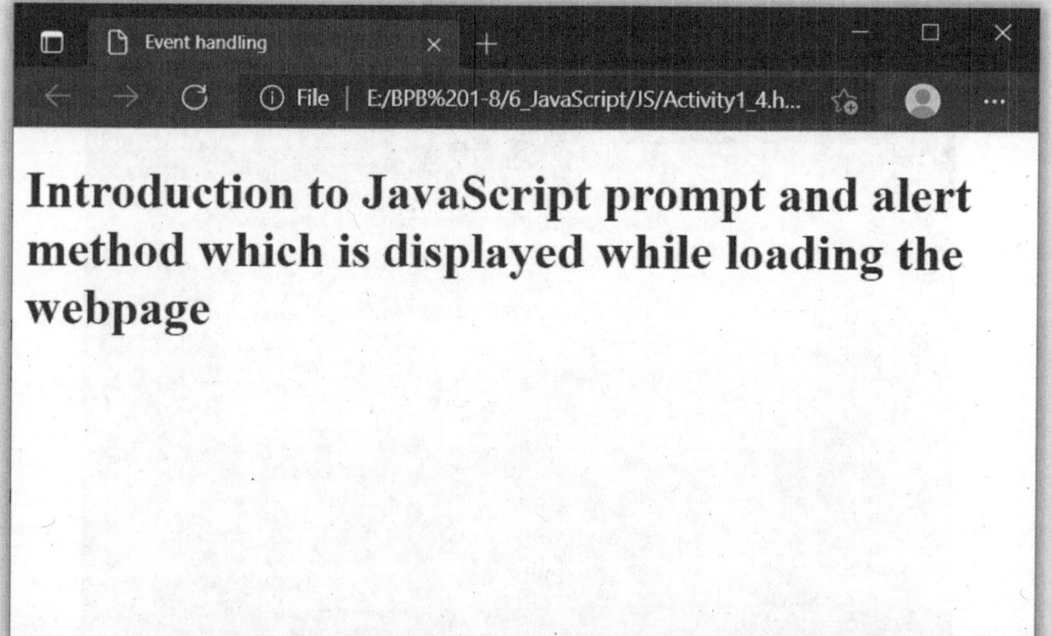

Figure 1.5(d): Output window for Activity 1.4

Practice Question

Use the JavaScript code to perform the following task for *figure 1.6(a)* to fill in the blanks given in *figure 1.6(b)*:

- **Heading of the page:** About Myself in red color, font style- Palatino.
- **Paragraph:** Write an introduction about yourself – background color pink, padding 20px, border 2px dashed blue color.

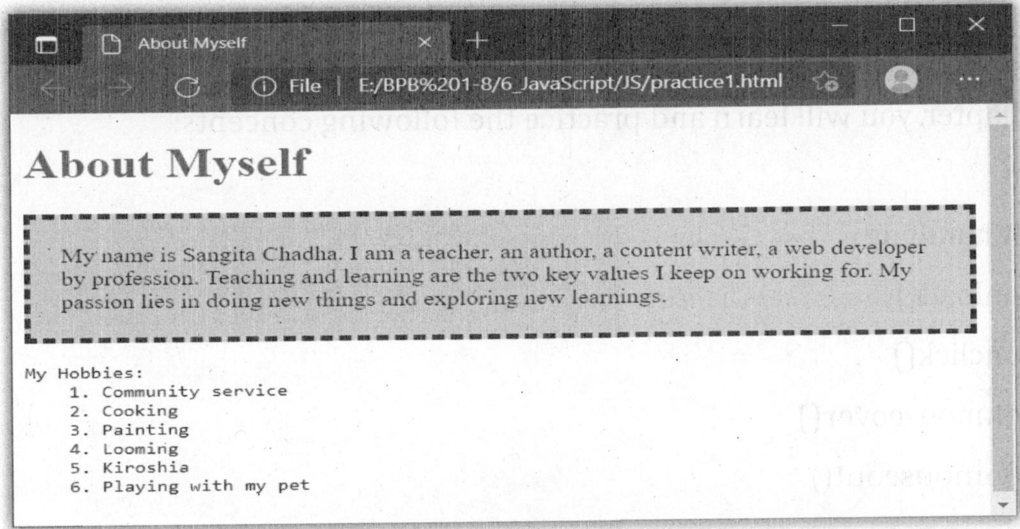

Figure 1.6(a): Output window for Practice

```
<!DOCTYPE html> <html lang="en">
<head> <title>About Myself</title> </head>
<body>
    <h1 id="heading">About Myself</h1>
    <p id="para">My name is Sangita Chadha. I am a teacher, an author, a
    content writer, a web developer by profession. Teaching and learning are
    the two key values I keep on working for. My passion lies in doing new
    things and exploring new learnings.  </p>
    <pre>My Hobbies:
    1. Community service
    2. Cooking
    3. Painting
    4. Looming
    5. Kiroshia
    6. Playing with my pet
    </pre>
    <script>
        document.getElementById("heading")._____.color="red";
        document.getElementById("heading").style._______="Palatino";
        document.getElementById("para")._____.backgroundColor="pink";
        document.getElementById("para").style.padding="____";
        document.getElementById("para").style._______="4px dashed blue";
    </script>
  </body>
```

Figure 1.6(b): Fill in the blanks to get the output as shown in figure 1.6(a)

Event Handling

Structure

In this chapter, you will learn and practice the following concepts:

- Event
- Event handling
  - onload()
  - onclick()
  - onmouseover()
  - onmouseout()

Learning Objective

At the end of this chapter, you will be able to:

- Display a message while loading the webpage
- Display or perform some simple activity by click on some button
- Change the properties of the HTML element by moving the cursor over the element and moving away from the cursor from that element

Event

When something happens, it is called an event. For example, when a webpage is loading, so a load is an event. If the user clicks on a button, this click is also an event. Other examples include moving the mouse over an element or moving out of an element, closing a window, etc.

Event handling

It is the action that needs to perform something while that event occurs. For example, if the user wishes to display a greeting message while loading a webpage. Then will use the **onload** event to display the message.

Let us perform some of the activities to understand how the event is handled to perform the specific task.

Activity 2.1

Write the code to display a welcome message on loading the webpage.

If there is a single statement to be displayed on loading the webpage then, you can directly call the **alert()** method in the HTML element as shown in *figure 2.1(a).*

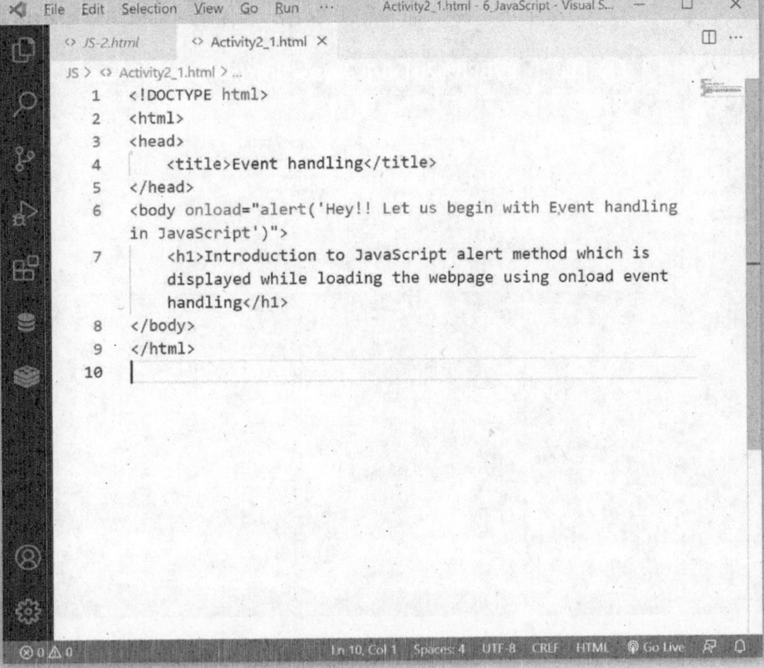

```
<!DOCTYPE html>
<html>
<head>
    <title>Event handling</title>
</head>
<body onload="alert('Hey!! Let us begin with Event handling
in JavaScript')">
    <h1>Introduction to JavaScript alert method which is
    displayed while loading the webpage using onload event
    handling</h1>
</body>
</html>
```

Figure 2.1(a): Code window for Activity 2.1

OR

There is one more way to call the **method()** using the function. You can write your functions in JavaScript within the <script></script> tag as shown in *figure 2.1(b)* and can be invoked any number of times.

```
<!DOCTYPE html>
<html>
<head>
    <title>Event handling</title>
    <script>
        function message()
        {
            alert("Hey!! Let us begin with Event handling in JavaScript")
        }
    </script>
</head>
<body onload="message()">
    <h1>Introduction to JavaScript alert method which is displayed while loading the webpage using onload event handling
    </h1>
</body>
</html>
```

Figure 2.1(b): Code window for Activity 2.1

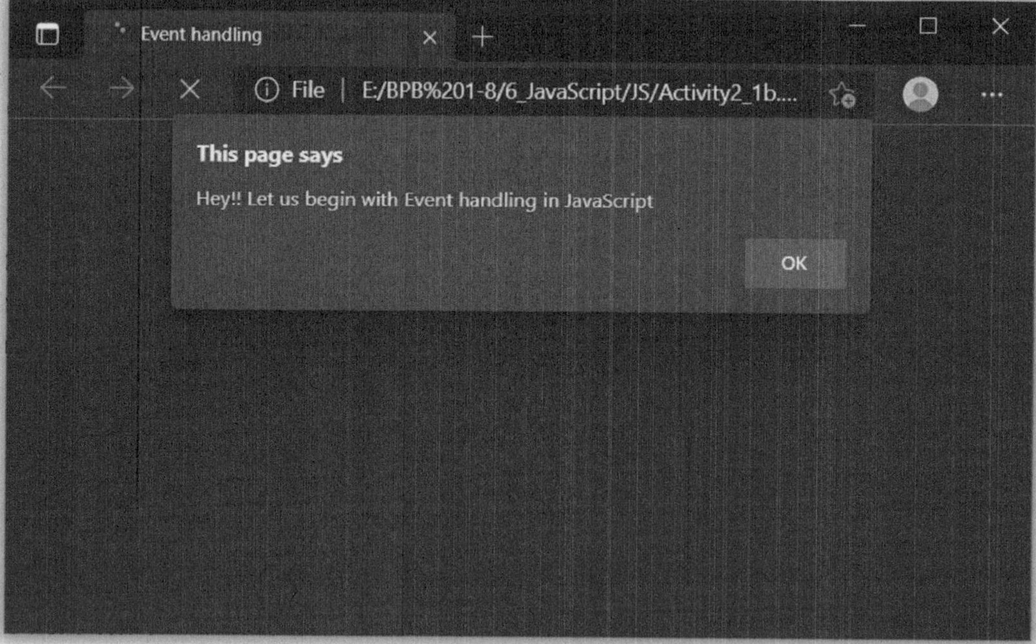

Figure 2.1(c): Output window for Activity 2.1

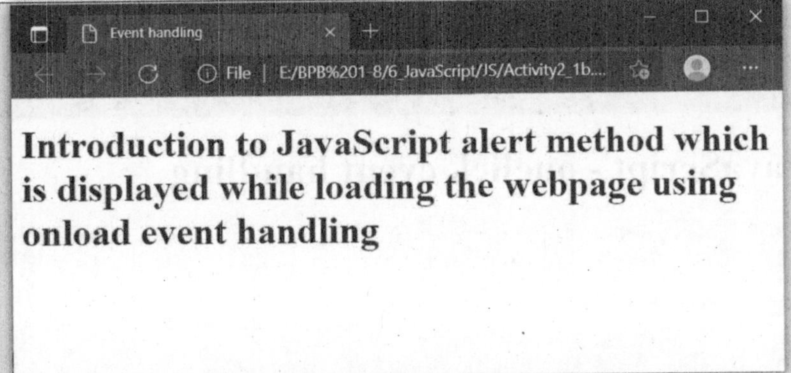

Figure 2.1(d): Output window for Activity 2.1

Info bot

Function is a set of statements that perform a particular task and can be called from the code "n" number of times.

Activity 2.2

To change the text color of the H1 element by clicking on the desired color name box and also change the background color to light blue.

To solve this, we created three functions that are going to be invoked when the user is going to click on the respective button for changing the color of the text.

```
<!DOCTYPE html>
<html>
<head> <title>Event handling</title>
    <script>
        function changer() {
        document.getElementById("para").style.color='red';
        document.getElementById("para").style.backgroundColor='lightblue';    }
        function changeb() {
        document.getElementById("para").style.color = 'blue';
        document.getElementById("para").style.backgroundColor = 'lightblue';   }
        function changeg() {
        document.getElementById("para").style.color = 'green';
        document.getElementById("para").style.backgroundColor = 'lightblue';   }
    </script>
</head>
<body>
    <h1> JavaScript - onclick event handling </h1>
    <p id="para">Let us create three buttons with Red, Blue and Green color names and then
    change the text color of this paragraph respectively by clicking on that button.  </p>
    <button value="red" onclick='changer()'>Red</button>
    <button value="blue" onclick='changeb()'>Blue</button>
    <button value="green" onclick='changeg()'>Green</button>
</body>
</html>
```

Figure 2.2(a): Code window for Activity 2.2

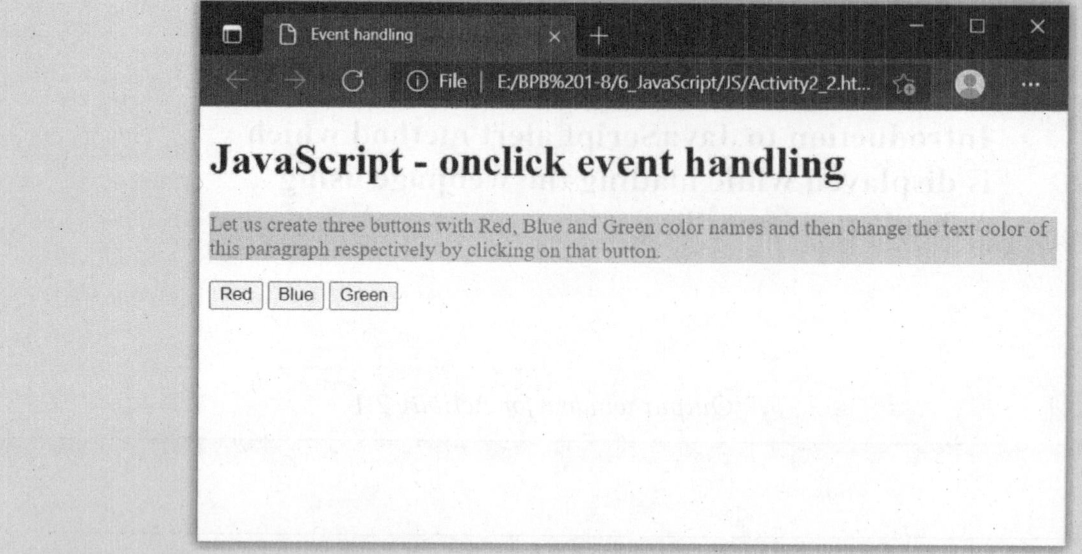

Figure 2.2(b): Output window for Activity 2.2

Activity 2.3

To change the text color of the paragraph to white and the background color to the one chosen from the drop-down menu by clicking on it.

```
<!DOCTYPE html>
<html>
<head>
    <title>Event handling-onclick</title>
    <script>
      function bkgdcolor()
      {
          var c= document.getElementById('col').value;
          document.getElementById('para').style.backgroundColor=c;
          document.getElementById('para').style.color='white';
      }
    </script>
</head>
<body>
    <h1> JavaScript - onclick event handling </h1>
    <p id="para">Let us create a drop-down list of favorite colours. When the user click
    on the colour then it sets that colour as the background colour of this paragraph and
    the colour of the text of this paragraph will be written with white. Select tag in
    HTML is used to create the drop-down list. </p>
    <select id='col' onclick="bkgdcolor()">
        <option value="Red">Red</option> <option value="Blue">Blue</option>
        <option value="Green">Green</option> <option value="Pink">Pink</option>
    </select>
</body>
</html>
```

Figure 2.3(a): Code window for Activity 2.3

Figure 2.3(b): Output window for Activity 2.3

Activity 2.4

To change the image dimensions, the height and width of 400 each when the cursor moves on the image and back to the original height and width of 100 after moving the cursor out of the image.

```
<!DOCTYPE html>
<html>
<head> <title>Event handling</title>
    <script>
      function incr()
      {
          document.getElementById("app").height="400";
          document.getElementById("app").width="400";
      }
      function decr()
      {
          document.getElementById('app').height = 100;
          document.getElementById('app').width = 100;
      }
    </script>
</head>
<body>
    <h1> JavaScript - onmouseover and onmouseout event handling </h1>
    <p>In this program, we will be adding one image of an apple using img tag of HTML.
    This image will be used with an id property in JavaScript function to change its
    height and width to 400 x 400. When the cursor moves away from the image, it will
    restore to the original height and width of 100x100. </p>
    <img src="E:\BPB 1-8\6_JavaScript\images\apple.jpg" alt="Image of an apple"
    height="100" width="100" id="app" onmouseover="incr()" onmouseout="decr()">
</body>
</html>
```

Figure 2.4(a): Code window for Activity 2.4

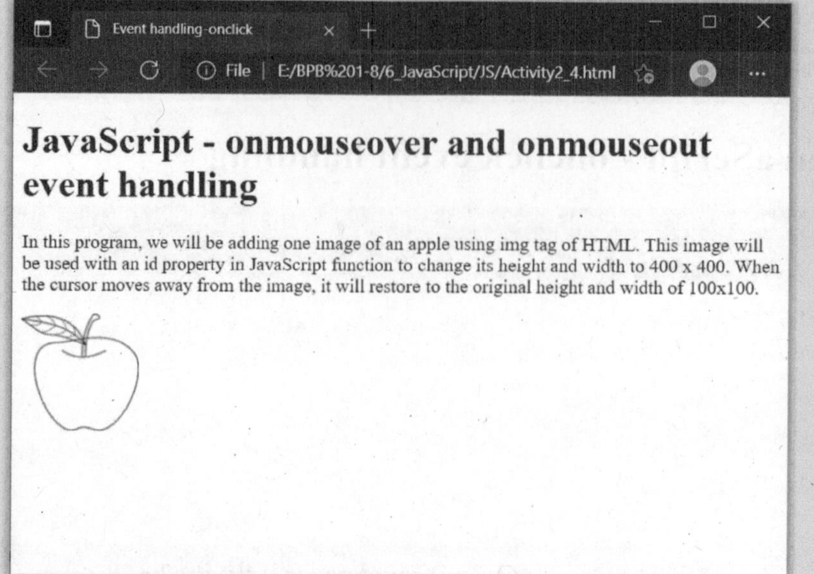

Figure 2.4(b): Output window for Activity 2.4

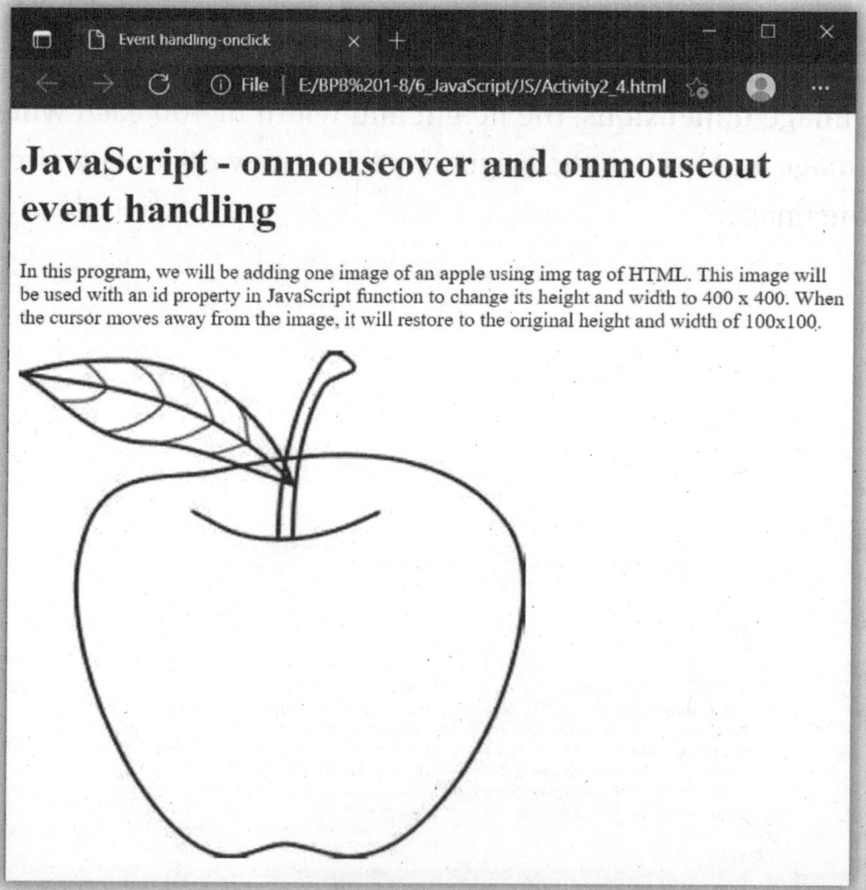

Figure 2.4(c): Output window for Activity 2.4 when the cursor moves over the apple

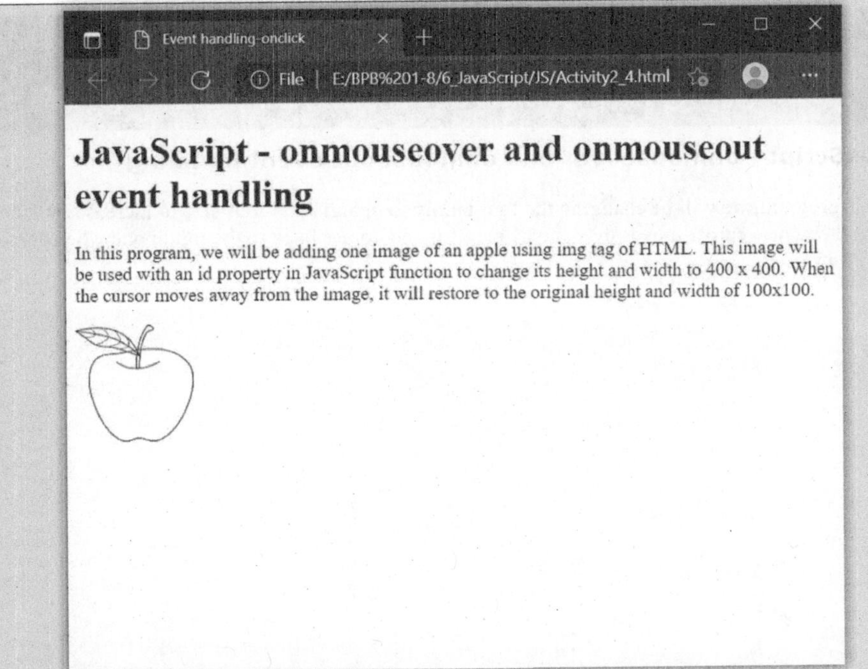

Figure 2.4(d): Output window for Activity 2.4 when the cursor moves away from the image of an apple

Activity 2.5

To change the font size to grow to 200% and font family to Georgia while moving the cursor on the <h1> element and back to 100% on moving out the mouse cursor.

```
<!DOCTYPE html>
<html>
<head>
    <title>Event handling</title>
    <script>
        function incr() {
            document.getElementById("heading").style.fontFamily = "Georgia";
            document.getElementById("heading").style.fontSize="200%";
        }
        function decr() {
            document.getElementById("heading").style.fontFamily = "verdana";
            document.getElementById("heading").style.fontSize="100%";
        }
    </script>
</head>
<body>
    <h1 id="heading" onmouseover="incr()" onmouseout="decr()" style="font-family: verdana;
    font-size: 100%;"> JavaScript - onmouseover and onmouseout event handling </h1>
    <p>In this program, we will be changing the font family to georgia and font-size to
    increase by 200% when the mouse curosr moves over the h1 element and comes back to the
    initial one when cursor moves away.</p>
</body>
</html>
```

Figure 2.5(a): Code window for Activity 2.5

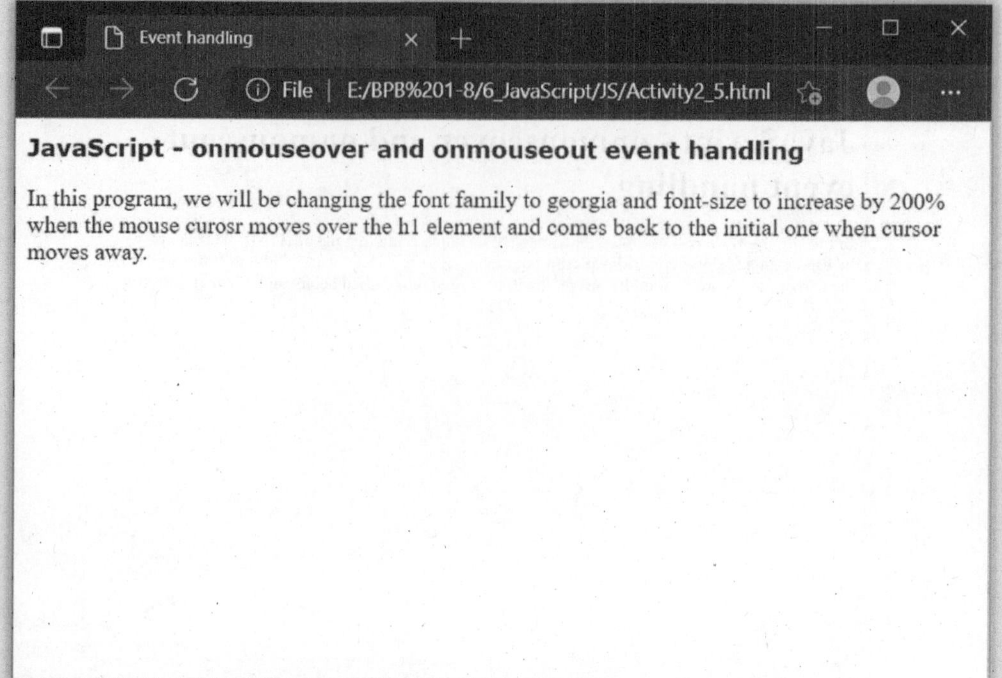

Figure 2.5(b): Output window for Activity 2.5 when the code is rendered on the browser window

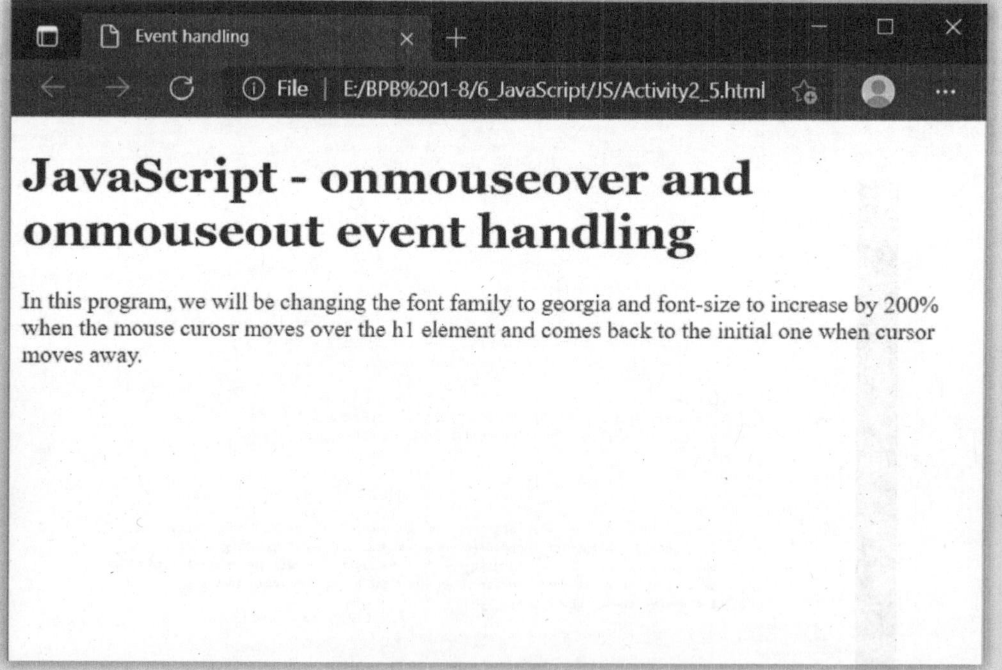

Figure 2.5(c): Output window for Activity 2.5 when the cursor moves over the heading which is created using the H1 tag in HTML

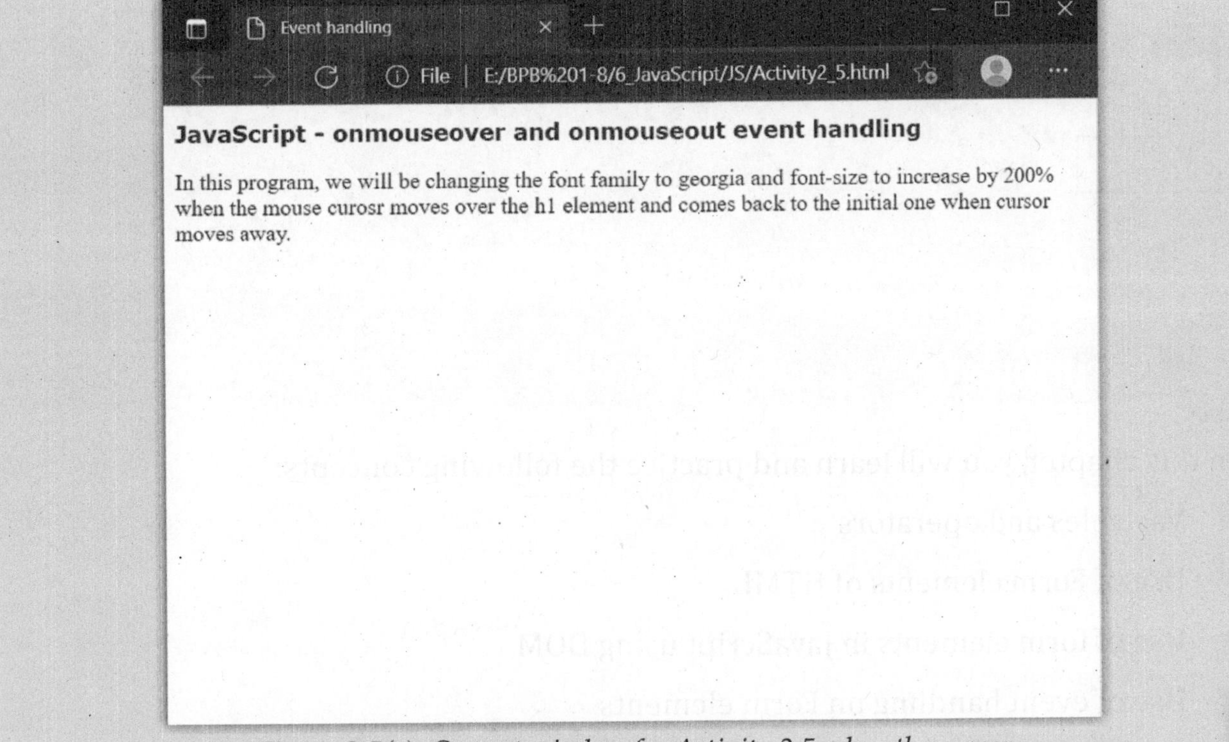

Figure 2.5(c): Output window for Activity 2.5 when the cursor moves away from the heading

Variables and Operators

Structure

In this chapter, you will learn and practice the following concepts:

- Variables and operators
- Use of Form elements of HTML
- Use of form elements in JavaScript using DOM
- Use of event handling on Form elements
- Use of external style sheet to change the look of the webpage and the HTML elements

Learning Objective

At the end of this chapter, you will be able to:

- Display a message while loading the webpage
- Display or perform some simple activity by click on some button
- Project – Simple JavaScript Calculator

A variable is a named memory location that stores the values that can be used later. A variable is a name that refers to a value that is declared with var keyword and an assignment statement to create new variables.

For example, if a number variable is to be created in JavaScript, then we will write:

```
var num=10;
```

JavaScript variables are case sensitive, for example, num and Num and NUM are different variables.

Operators are special symbols that represent computation which is applied on operand(s), which can be values or variables. An expression is created when operators are applied to operands. The same operator can behave differently when applied to different types of data values.

Operators are categorized as:

- Arithmetic
- Relational
- Logical
- Assignment

Arithmetic Operators are used with numeric values to perform common mathematical operations.

Arithmetic operators are:

Operator	Operation
+	Addition
-	Subtraction
/	Division
*	Multiplication
%	Modulus (Remainder)
**	Exponent (power)

Activity 3.1

To perform addition operations while taking input from the user using **prompt()** method and displaying the output using the **alert()** method.

In this code, we will see how the data is taken from the prompt method. The **parseInt()** method is used to convert the number taken in string format to numeric format.

Info bot

prompt() method returns the data in the form of a string value.

```
<!DOCTYPE html>
<html lang="en">
<head>
    <title>Addition operation</title>
</head>
<body>
    <h1>Arithmetic Operations</h1>
    <script>
        var num1 = parseInt(prompt("Enter first number "))
        var num2 = parseInt(prompt("Enter second number "))
        var c = num1 + num2
        alert("Sum of " + num1 + " & " + num2 + " = " + c)
    </script>
</body>
</html>
```

Figure 3.1(a): Code window for Activity 3.1

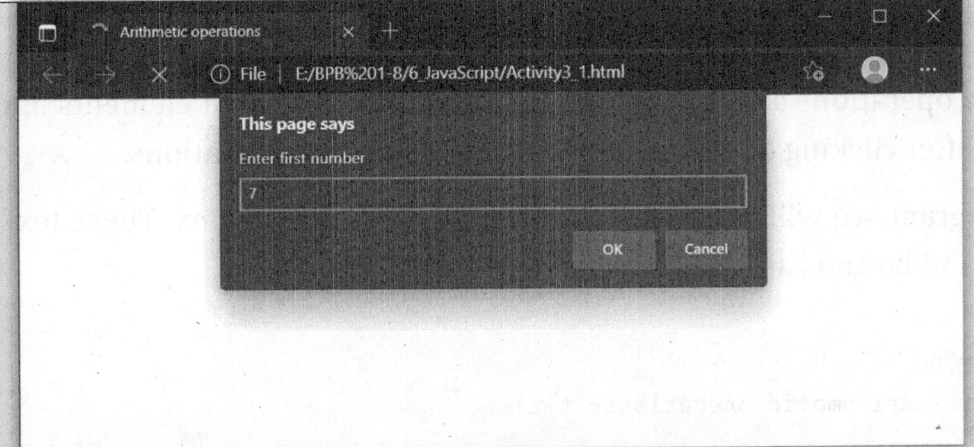

Figure 3.1(b): Code window for Activity 3.1

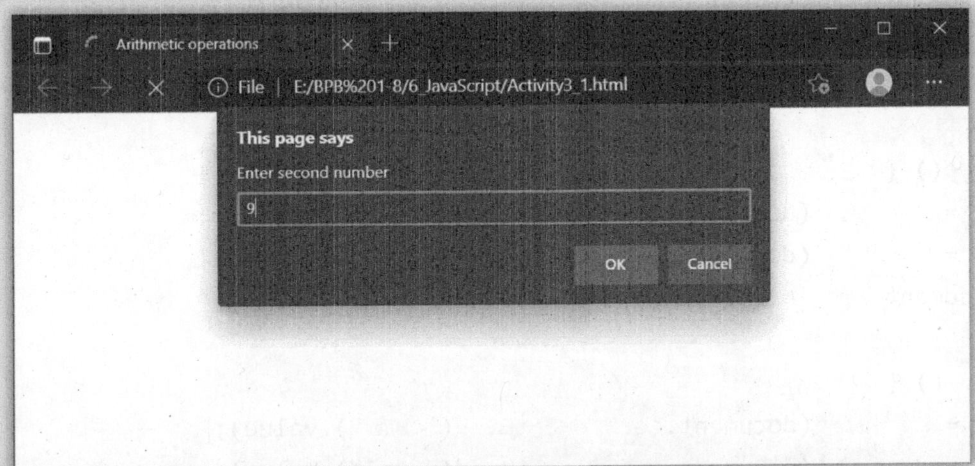

Figure 3.1(c): Code window for Activity 3.1

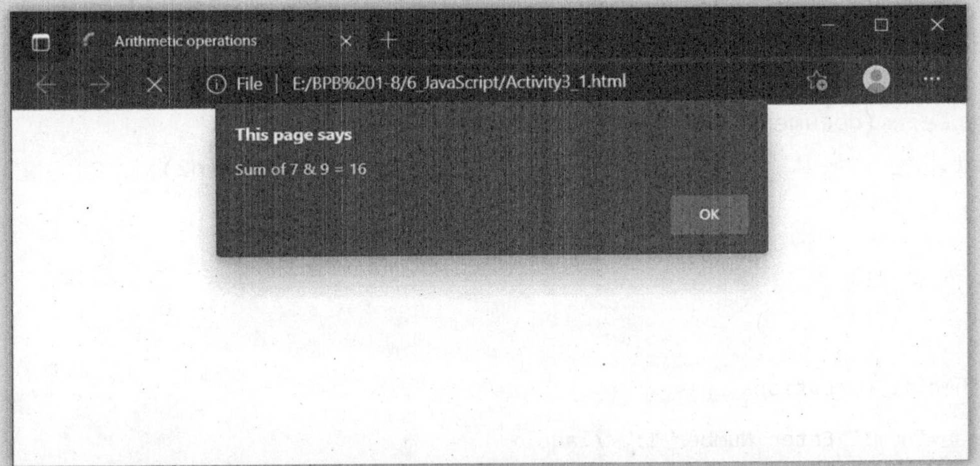

Figure 3.1(d): Code window for Activity 3.1

Activity 3.2

Arithmetic operations after taking input from the HTML form elements and display the result after clicking on the buttons for the respective operations.

In this program, we will make the user give input in the textbox. These text box and the command buttons are the form elements of HTML.

```
<!DOCTYPE html>
<html lang="en">
<head> <title>Arithmetic operations</title>
<script>
function add(){
        n1=parseInt(document.getElementById("num1").value);
        n2=parseInt(document.getElementById("num2").value);
        document.getElementById("result").value=n1+n2;
    }
function sub() {
        n1 = parseInt(document.getElementById("num1").value);
        n2 = parseInt(document.getElementById("num2").value);
        document.getElementById("result").value = n1 - n2;
    }
function mul() {
        n1 = parseInt(document.getElementById("num1").value);
        n2 = parseInt(document.getElementById("num2").value);
        document.getElementById("result").value = n1 * n2;
    }
function div() {
    n1 = parseInt(document.getElementById("num1").value);
    n2 = parseInt(document.getElementById("num2").value);
    document.getElementById("result").value = parseFloat(n1 / n2);
    }
</script>
</head>
<body>
    <h1>Arithmetic Operations</h1>
    <label for="num1">Enter Number 1: </label>
    <input type="text" id="num1"> <br> <br>
```

```
    <label for="num2">Enter Number 2: </label>
    <input type="text" id="num2"> <br> <br>
    <label for="result">Result: </label>
    <input type="text" id="result" disabled> <br> <br>
    <input type="button" value="+" onclick="add()">
    <input type="button" value="-" onclick="sub()">
    <input type="button" value="x" onclick="mul()">
    <input type="button" value="/" onclick="div()">
</body>
</html>
```

Figure 3.2(a): Code window for Activity 3.2

Addition operation by clicking on Add button

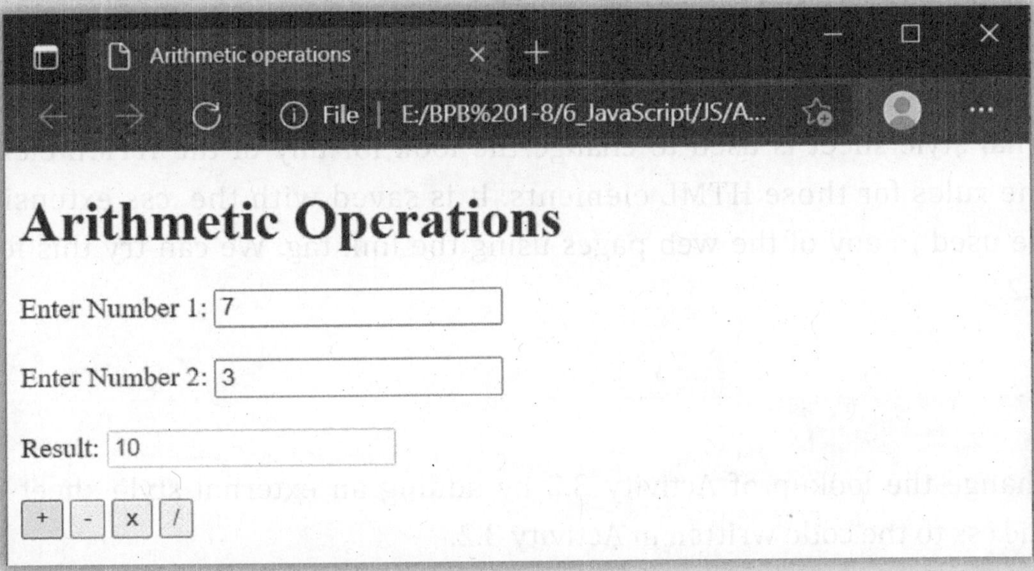

Figure 3.2(b): Output window for Activity 3.2

Division operation by clicking on the Divide button

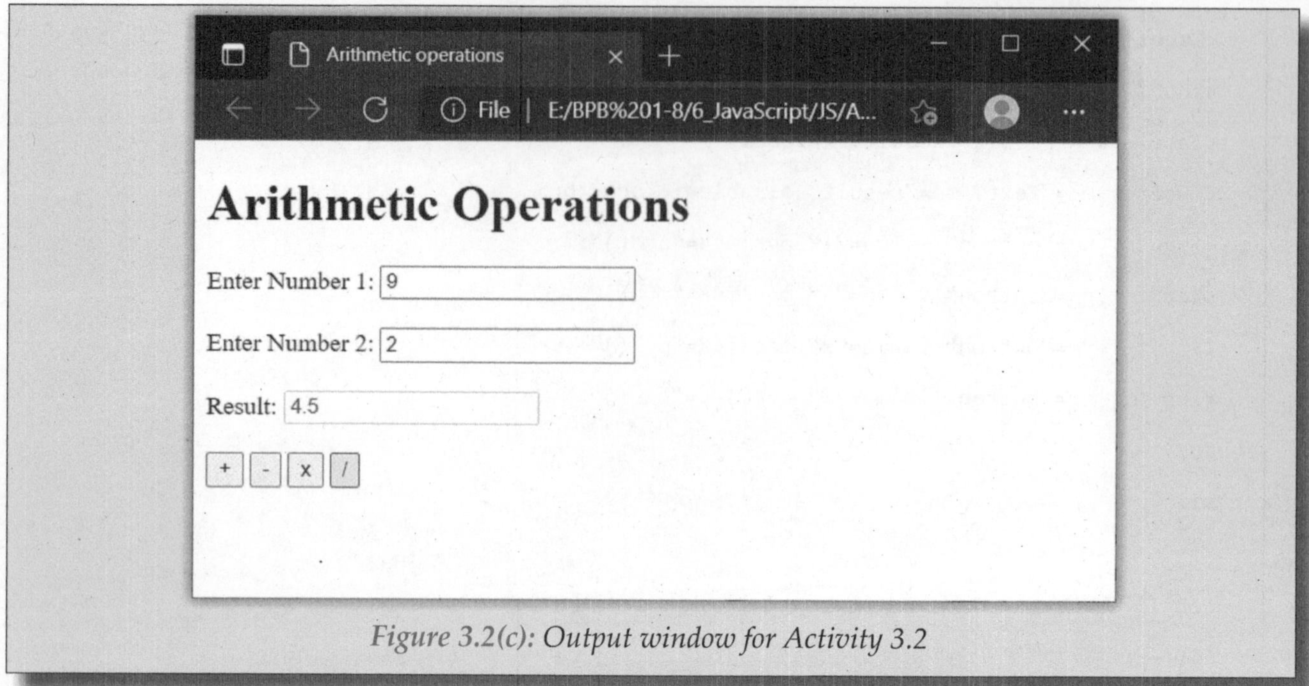

Figure 3.2(c): Output window for Activity 3.2

The first two textboxes can be allowed to take input from the user. But the third textbox should not be allowed to take the input from the user. So, the third text box is having the attribute disabled so that the user can't interact with this textbox.

Info bot

parseFloat converts and returns the numbers in the floating-point format i.e., in decimal format.

The external style sheet is used to change the look for any of the HTML elements. It creates the rules for those HTML elements. It is saved with the .css extension. This file can be used in any of the web pages using the link tag. We can try this feature in Activity 3.2.

Activity 3.3

Let us change the lookup of Activity 3.2 by adding an external style sheet named arithmetic.css to the code written in Activity 3.2.

Add the following line statement in the <Head></Head> section of code in Activity 3.2

```
<link rel="stylesheet" href="arithmetic.css">
```

```
<!DOCTYPE html>
<html lang="en">
<head> <title>Arithmetic operations</title>
    <link rel="stylesheet" href="arithmetic.css">
<script>
function add(){
        n1=parseInt(document.getElementById("num1").value);
        n2=parseInt(document.getElementById("num2").value);
        document.getElementById("result").value=n1+n2;
    }
function sub() {
        n1 = parseInt(document.getElementById("num1").value);
        n2 = parseInt(document.getElementById("num2").value);
        document.getElementById("result").value = n1 - n2;
    }
function mul() {
        n1 = parseInt(document.getElementById("num1").value);
        n2 = parseInt(document.getElementById("num2").value);
        document.getElementById("result").value = n1 * n2;
    }
```

Figure 3.3(a): Code window of adding the CSS link for Activity 3.2

Step 1: Click on the New file.

Click on add a new file and then write the filename.

Step 2: Type in the file name as arithmetic.css.

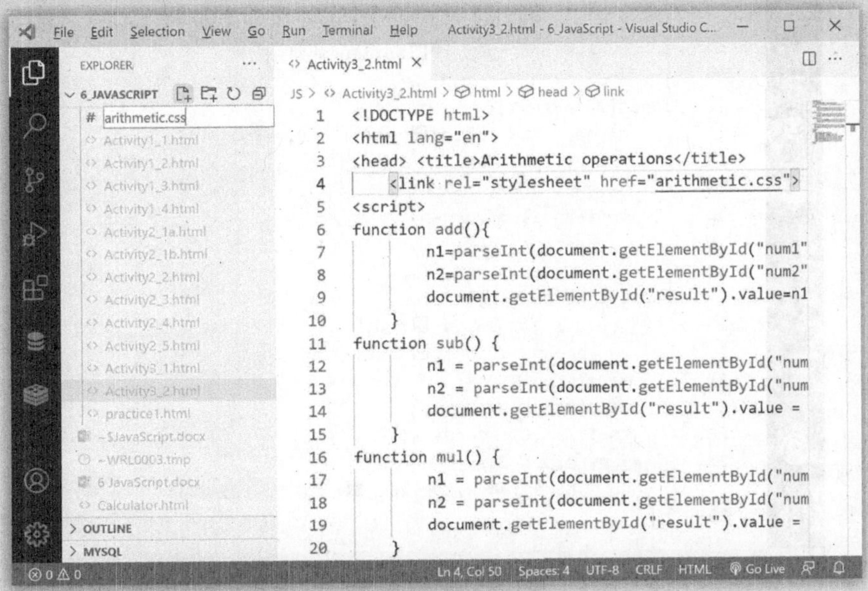

Figure 3.3(b): Click on New File and then the filename

Step 3: Hit the enter key.

Here we will write the CSS rules as shown in figure 3.3(d)

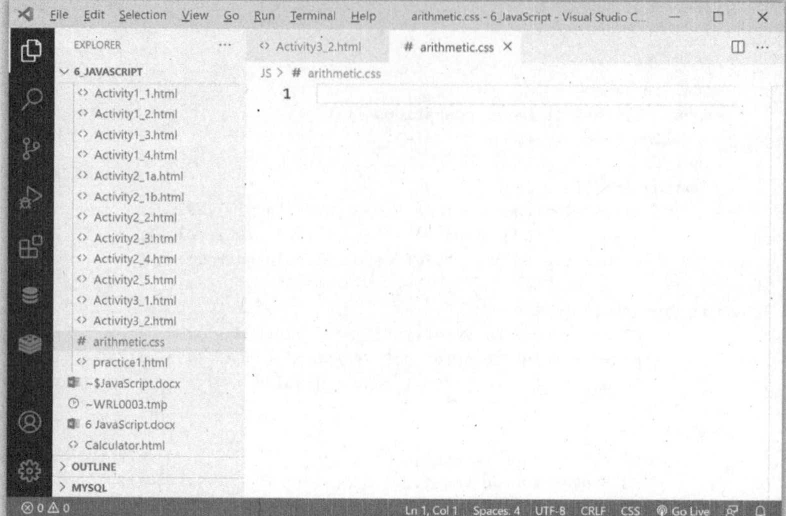

Figure 3.3(c): CSS file is created and now start coding

```
body{
    background-color: azure;
    text-align: center;
    font-family: verdana;
    font-size: 24px;
}
h1{
    background-color: antiquewhite;
}
input[type=text]{
    border: 2px solid rgb(111, 0, 255);
    width: 50%;
    height: 40px;
    font-family: verdana;
    font-size: 24px;
}
input[type=button]{
    border: 2px solid red;
    background-color: aqua;
    margin: 5px 2px;
    padding: 20px 32px;
    font-family: verdana;
    font-size: 24px;
    box-shadow: 4px 2px 2px rgb(48, 45, 45);
}
```

Figure 3.3(d): Code window of CSS file for Activity 3.3 – arithmetic.css

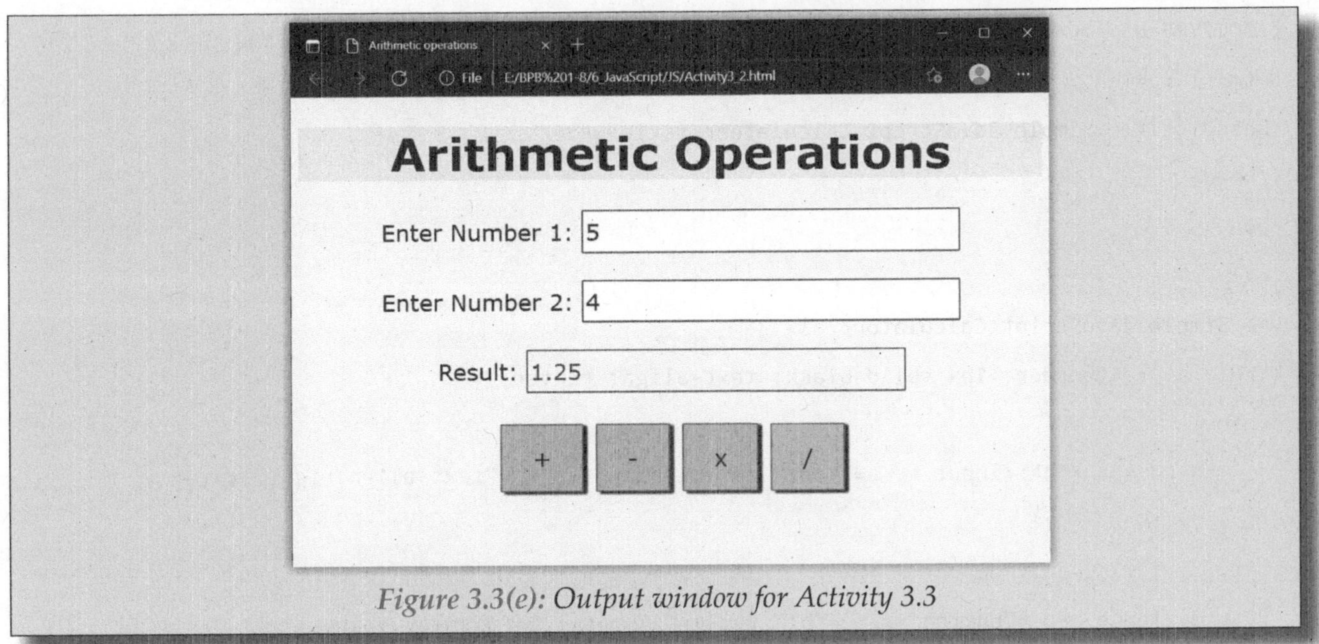

Figure 3.3(e): Output window for Activity 3.3

PROJECT

A Simple Calculator

Version 1: Without the CSS file

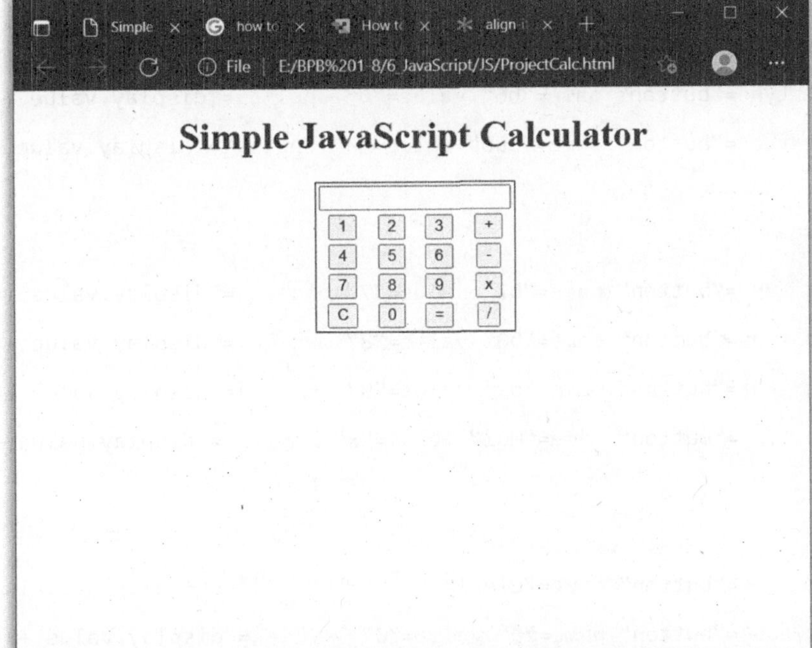

Figure 3.4(a): Output window for Project

```
<!DOCTYPE html>
<html lang="en">
<head> <title>Simple JavaScript Calculator</title>
</head>
<body>
<center>
<h1>Simple JavaScript Calculator</h1>
<table style="border: 1px solid black; text-align: center;">
<tr>
    <td colspan="4"><input type="text" id="display" style="text-align:right"></td>
</tr>
<tr>
    <td><input type="button" name="b1" value="1" onclick="display.value += '1'"></td>
    <td><input type="button" name="b2" value="2" onclick="display.value += '2'"></td>
    <td><input type="button" name="b3" value="3" onclick="display.value += '3'"></td>
    <td><input type="button" name="Add" value="+" onclick="display.value += ' + '"></td>
</tr>
<tr>
    <td><input type="button" name="b4" value="4" onclick="display.value += '4'"></td>
    <td><input type="button" name="b5" value="5" onclick="display.value += '5'"></td>
    <td><input type="button" name="b6" value="6" onclick="display.value += '6'"></td>
    <td><input type="button" name="Sub" value="-" onclick="display.value += ' - '"></td>
</tr>
<tr>
    <td><input type="button" name="b7" value="7" onclick="display.value += '7'"></td>
    <td><input type="button" name="b8" value="8" onclick="display.value += '8'"></td>
    <td><input type="button" name="b9" value="9" onclick="display.value += '9'"></td>
    <td><input type="button" name="Mul" value="x" onclick="display.value += ' * '"></td>
</tr>
<tr>
    <td><input type="button" name="Clear" value="C" onclick="display.value = ''"></td>
    <td><input type="button" name="0" value="0" onclick="display.value += '0'"></td>
    <td><input type="button" name="Equal" value="="
```

```
            onclick=”display.value = eval(display.value)”></td>

    <td><input type=”button” name=”Div” value=”/” onclick=”display.value += ‘ / ‘”></td>

</tr>

</table> </center>

</body> </html>
```

Figure 3.4(b): Code window for Project

Version 2:

Let us create the CSS file to change the look of the Calculator and add only one line of code to the HTML file to include the CSS file.

Create the calc.css file as shown in figure 3.5(a) and write one line of code in the code given in figure 3.4(b) as shown in figure 3.5(b) using the link tag.

```
body{
    margin: 20px;
    background-color: azure;

}
table td{
    background-color: aqua;
    padding: 15px;
}
input[type=button]{
    font-size: 20px;
    padding: 20px;
    background-color: antiquewhite;
    box-shadow: 4px 4px 4px rgb(71, 66, 66);
    border-radius: 50%;
}
input[type=text]{
    padding: 5%;
    width: 90%;
    font-size: 20px;
}
```

Figure 3.5(a): Code window for calc.css

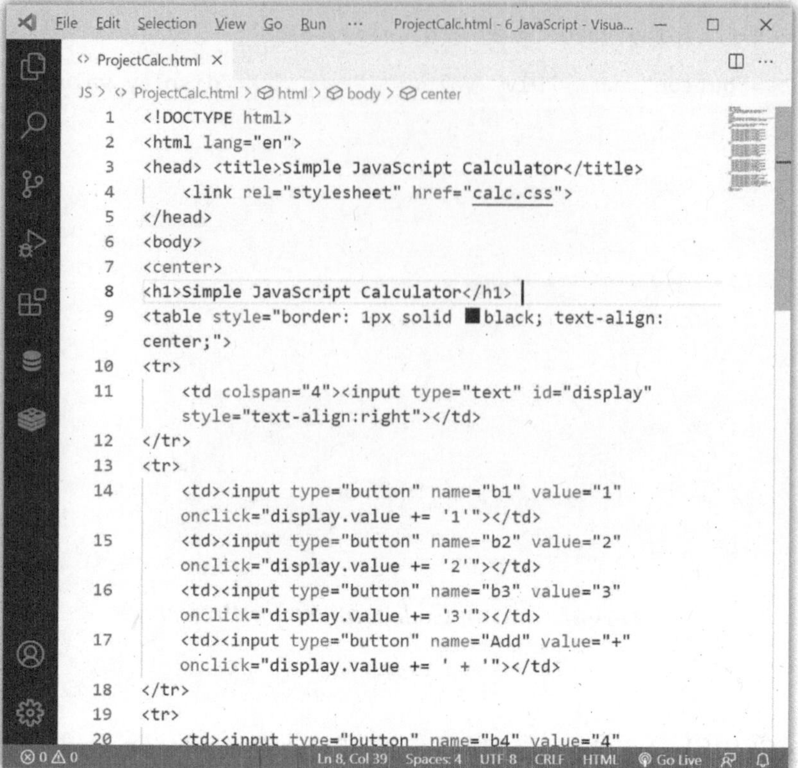

Figure 3.5(b): One line of code written within the head tag needs to be added in the head tag of the previous code given in figure 3.4(b)

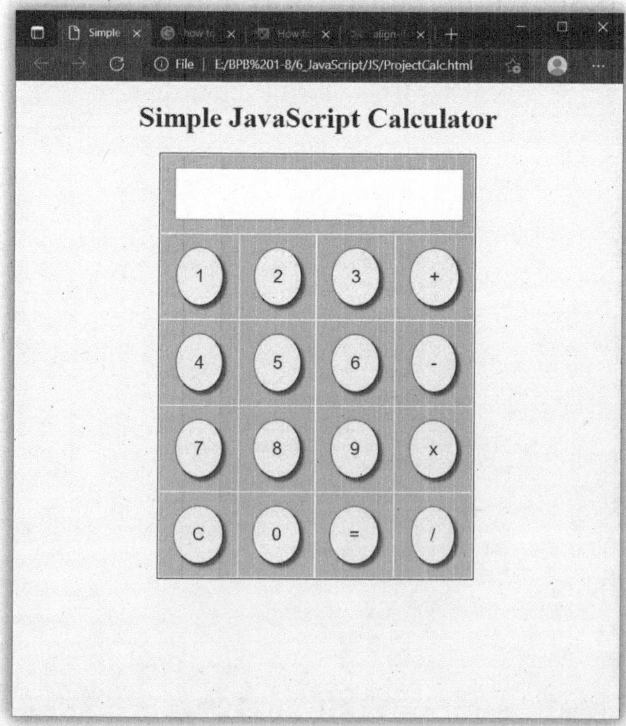

Figure 3.5(c): Output window for Version 2 of Project Calculator

Taking Decisions

Structure

In this chapter, you will learn and practice the following concepts:

- Relational operators
- Use of conditions of different types
- Use of Form elements of HTML with conditions
- Use of external style sheet to change the look of the webpage and the HTML elements

Learning Objective

At the end of this chapter, you will be able to:

- Display a greeting message while loading the webpage depending upon the day of the hour
- Display or perform some action based on some condition
- Display or perform some simple activity by click on some button while checking the conditions along with it
- Project –Real-time digital clock

Conditions are also known as selection statements for making decisions and branching of the flow of control; that is, choosing between two or more alternative paths.

In JavaScript, we have

- if statement
- if ... else statement
- if ... else if... else statement

When there is only one condition then use the **if** statement. When you have two options then go for using the **if ... else** statement and when you have more than two options to choose from then try using **if ... else if ... else if ... else** block of code.

Relational Operators

It compares the values. It either returns True or False according to the condition.

Operator	Operation
>	Greater than
<	Less than
= =	Equal to
!=	Not equal to
>=	Greater than or equal to
<=	Less than or equal to

Activity 4.1

Take the number from the user using the prompt() method and display whether the number is even or odd using the alert() method.

```
<!DOCTYPE html>
<html lang="en">
<head>
    <title>Conditions</title>
</head>
<body>
    <script>
        var num=parseInt(prompt("Enter the number to check for even or odd? "))
        if (num % 2 == 0)
        {
            alert(num + " is an even number")
        }
        else
        {
            alert(num + " is an odd number")
        }
    </script>
</body>
</html>
```

Figure 4.1(a): Code window for Activity 4.1

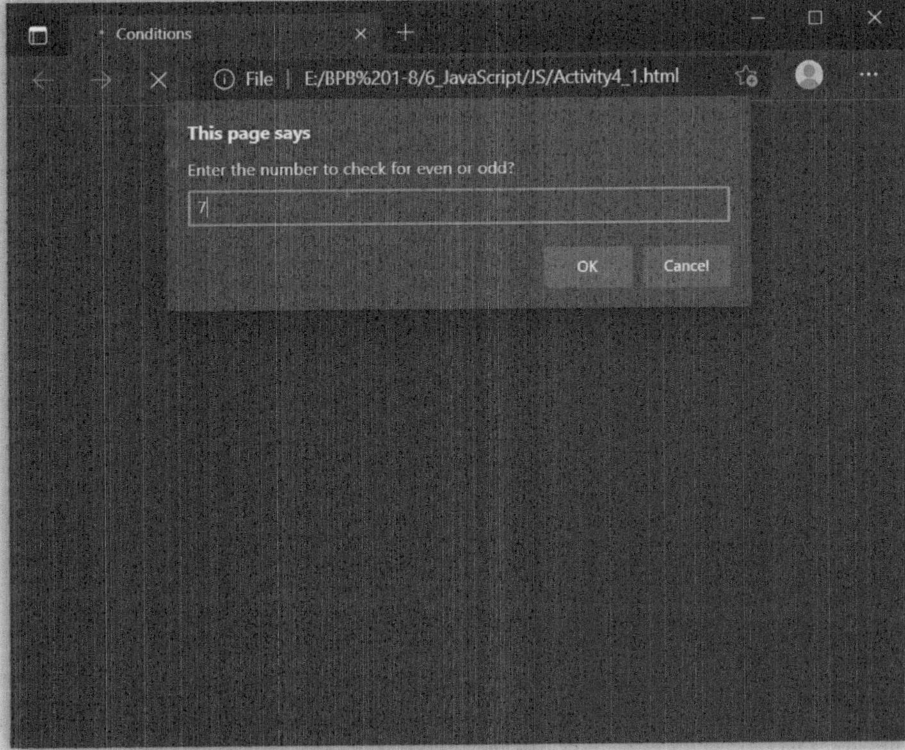

Figure 4.1(b): Output window for Activity 4.1

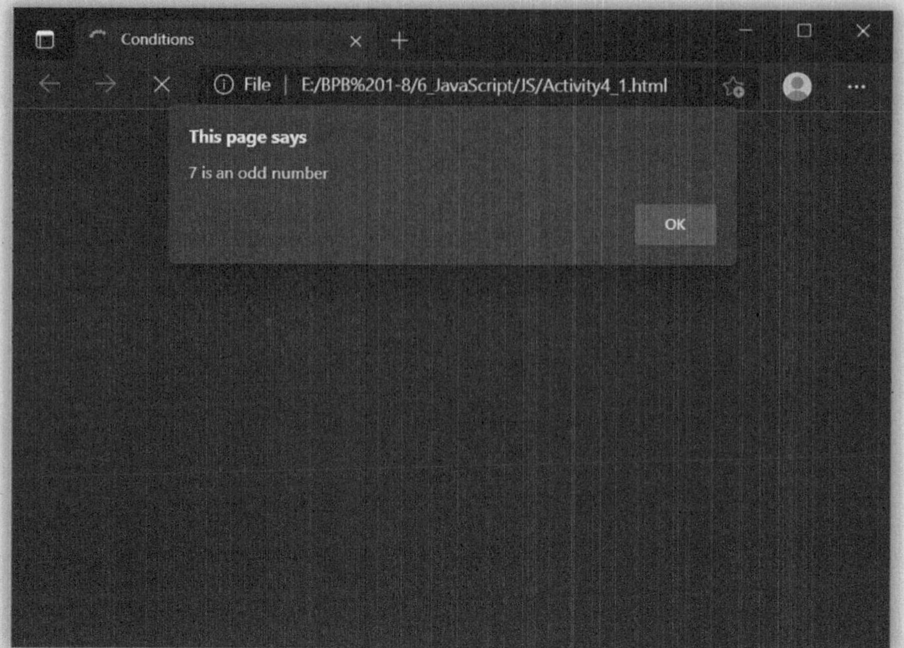

Figure 4.1(c): Output window for Activity 4.1

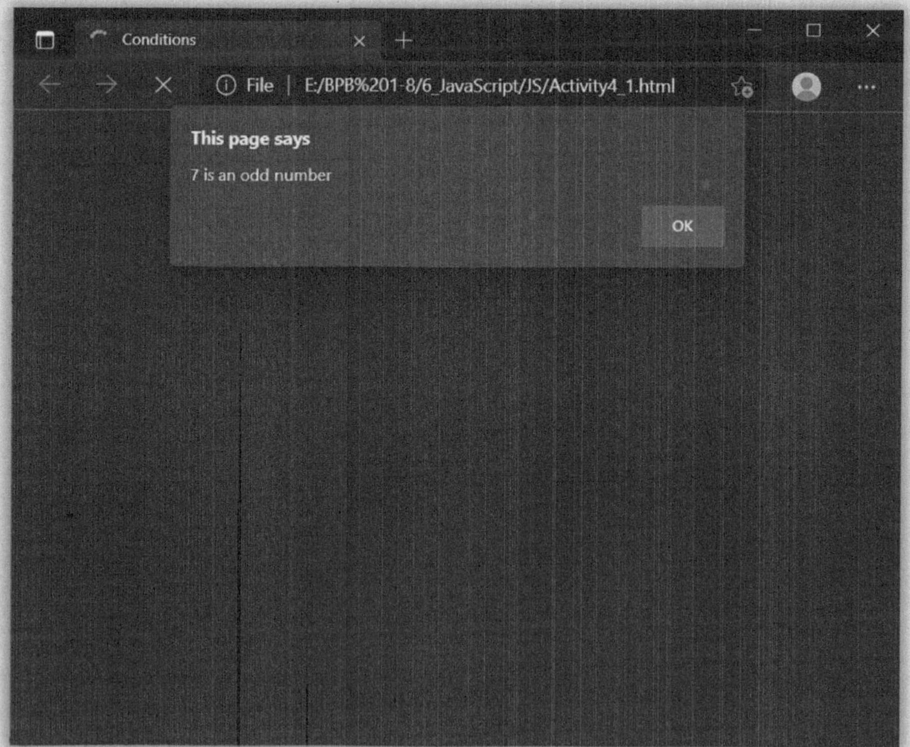

Figure 4.1(d): Output window for Activity 4.1

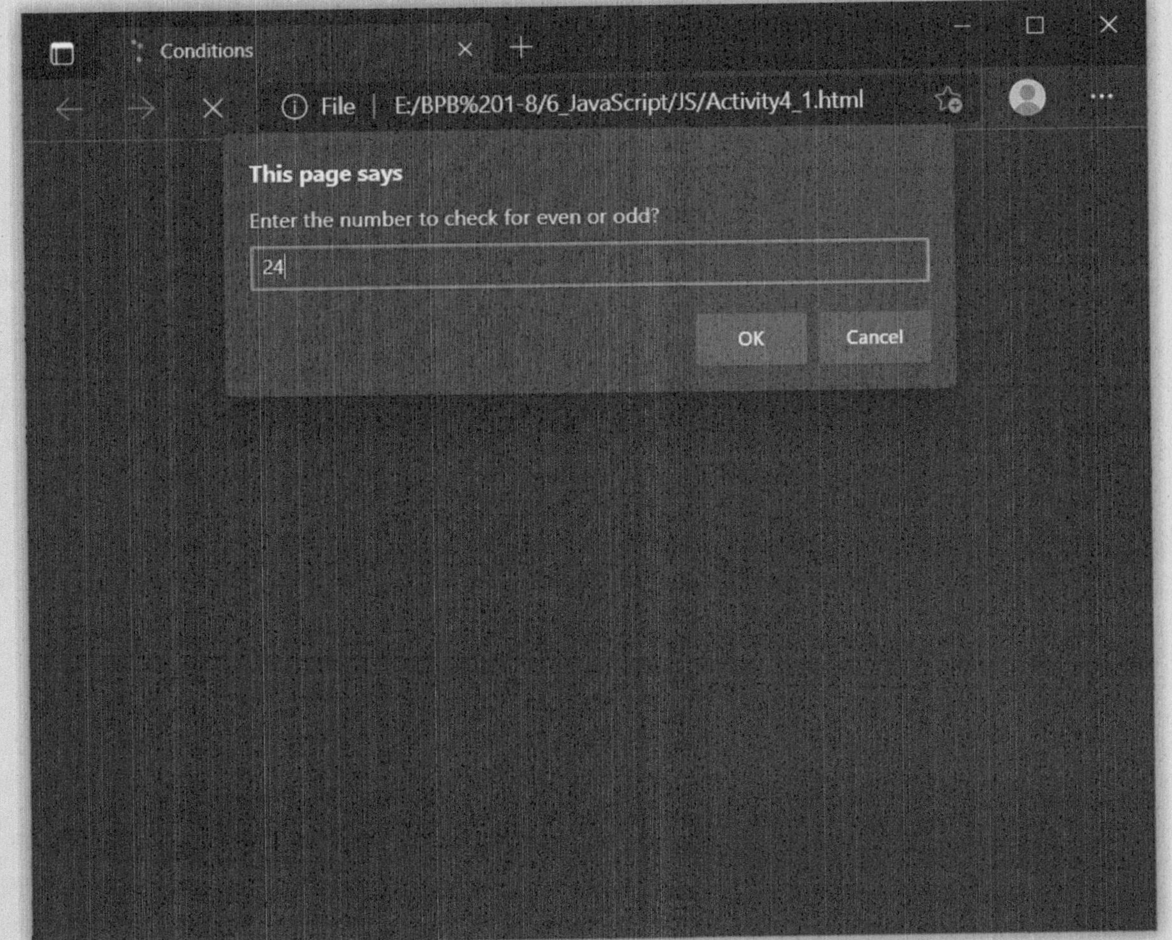

Figure 4.1(e): Output window for Activity 4.1

Activity 4.2

Read the name and choose Gender from the input form elements in the HTML. Display an appropriate message depending upon the gender selected from the radio/options button.

If the user enters name as XYZ and selects Male as gender then the output would be Hello, Mr. XYX and if the user enters name as ABC and selects Female as gender then the output would be Hello, Ms. ABC

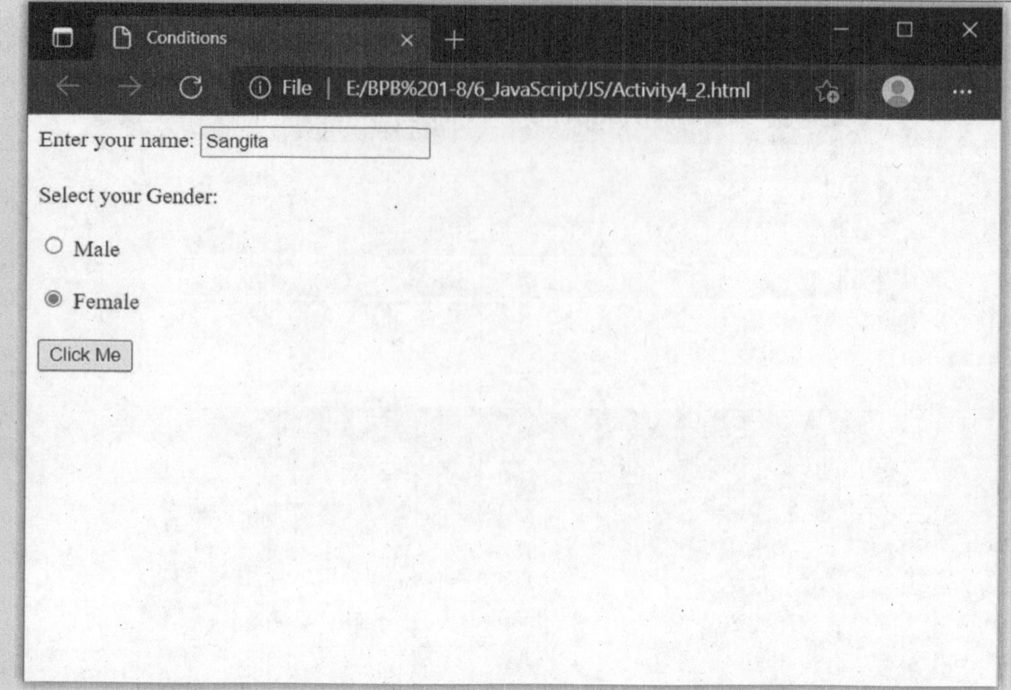

Figure 4.2(a): Output window for Activity 4.2

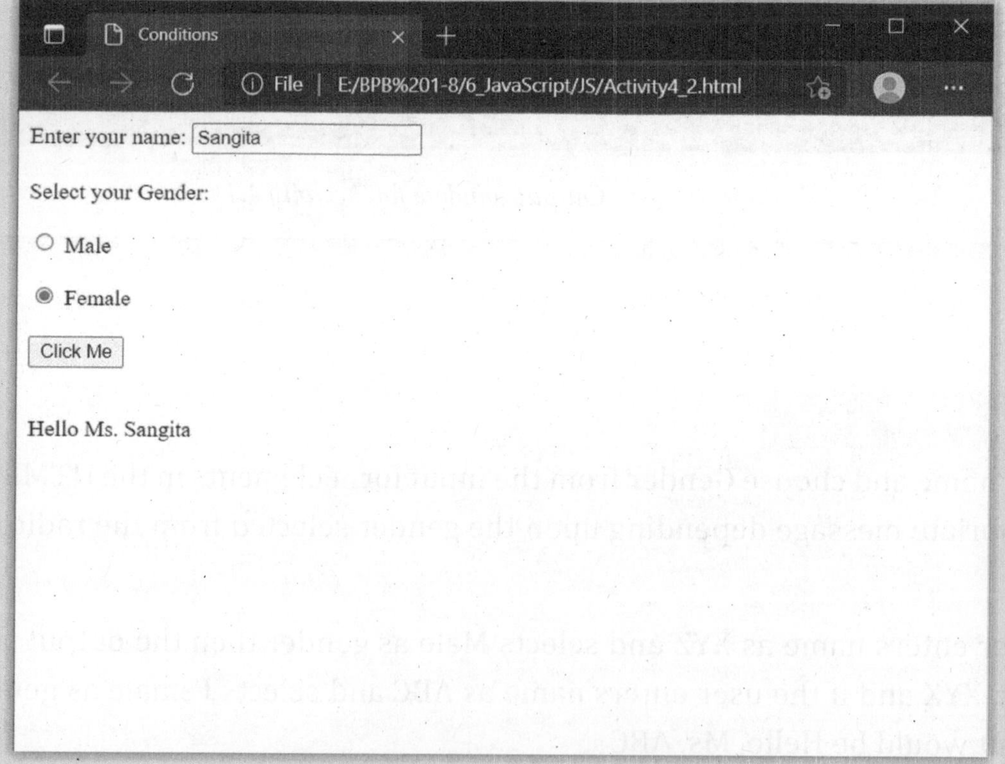

Figure 4.2(b): Output window for Activity 4.2

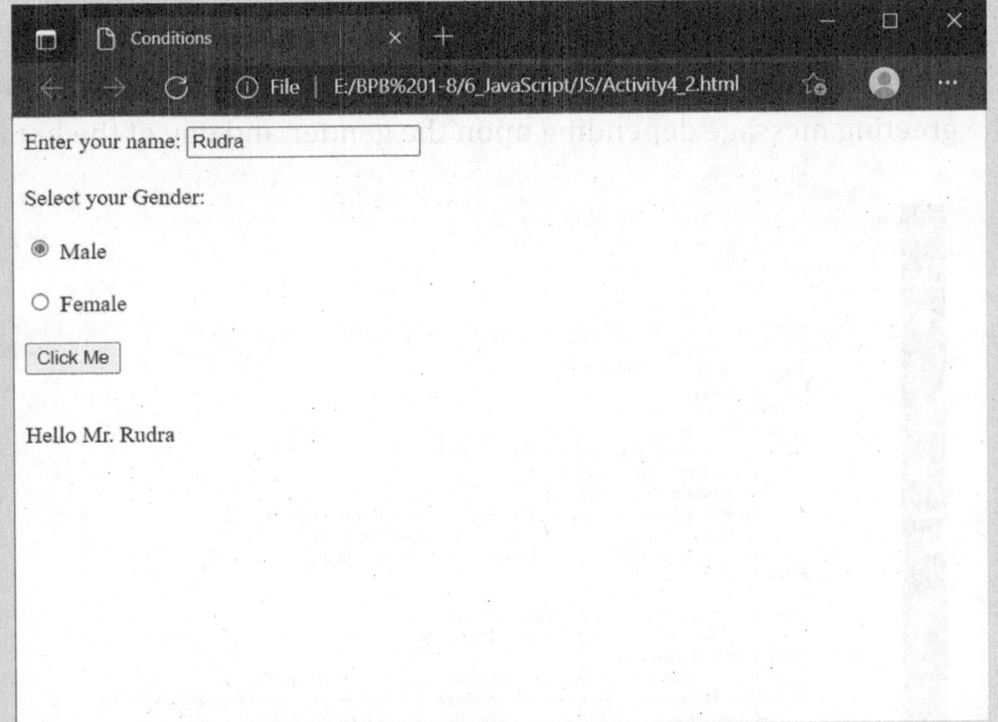

Figure 4.2(c): Output window for Activity 4.2

```
<!DOCTYPE html>
<html lang="en">
<head> <title>Conditions</title>
    <script>
        function message()
        {
            var n=document.getElementById('uname').value;
            if (document.getElementById("Male").checked==true)
             {  var g = 'Mr. '; }
             else if(document.getElementById("Female").checked==true)
             {  var g = 'Ms. '; }
            document.getElementById("para").innerHTML="Hello " + g + n;
        }
    </script>
</head>
<body>
    <label for="uname">Enter your name: </label>
    <input type="text" name="username" id="uname"> <br> <br>
    Select your Gender: <br><br>
    <input type="radio" name="gender" id="Male" value="Male"> Male <br><br>
    <input type="radio" name="gender" id="Female" value="Female"> Female  <br>
    <br>
    <input type="button" onclick="message()" value="Click Me"> <br><br>
    <p id="para"></p>
</body>
</html>
```

Figure 4.2(d): Code window for Activity 4.2

Activity 4.3

Read the name and choose the gender from the input form elements in the HTML. Display the greeting message depending upon the gender and day of the hour.

```html
<!DOCTYPE html>
<html lang="en">
<head> <title>Condition</title> </head>
<script>
function message() {
    var t = new Date().getHours();
    var greeting;
    if (t < 12) { greeting = "Good morning! "; }
    else if (t < 16) { greeting = "Good afternoon! "; }
    else if (t < 20) { greeting = "Good evening! "; }
    else { greeting = "Good night! "; }
    var n = document.getElementById('uname').value;
    if (document.getElementById("Male").checked == true) { var g = 'Mr. '; }
    else if (document.getElementById("Female").checked == true) { var g = 'Ms. '; }
    document.getElementById("para").innerHTML = greeting + g + n; }
</script>
<body>
    <label for="uname">Enter your Name: </label>
    <input type="text" name="username" id="uname"> <br> <br>
    Select your Gender: <br><br>
    <input type="radio" name="gender" id="Male" value="Male"> Male <br><br>
    <input type="radio" name="gender" id="Female" value="Female"> Female <br> <br>
    <input type="button" onclick="message()" value="Click Me"> <br><br>
    <p id="para"></p>
</body>
</html>
```

Figure 4.3(a): Code window for Activity 4.3

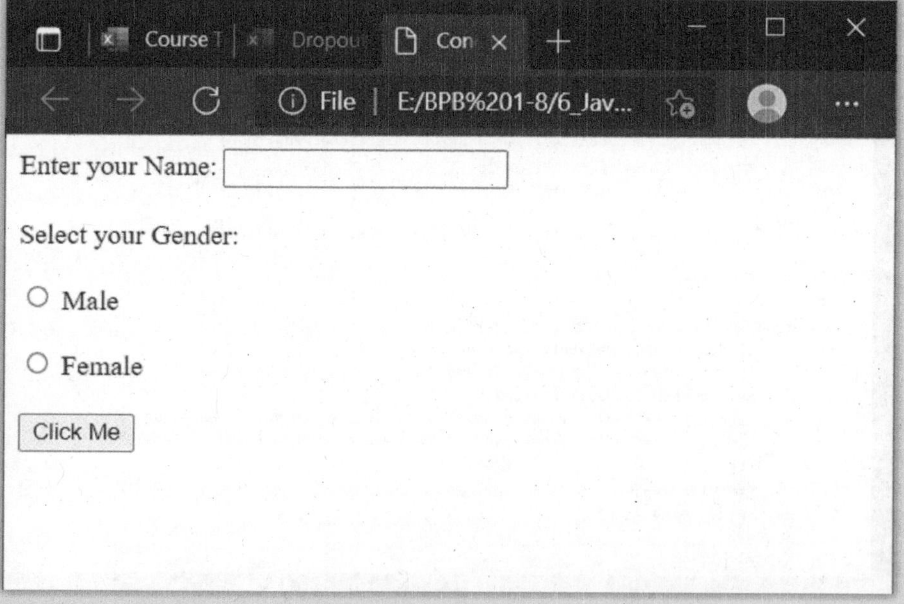

Figure 4.3(b): Output window for Activity 4.3

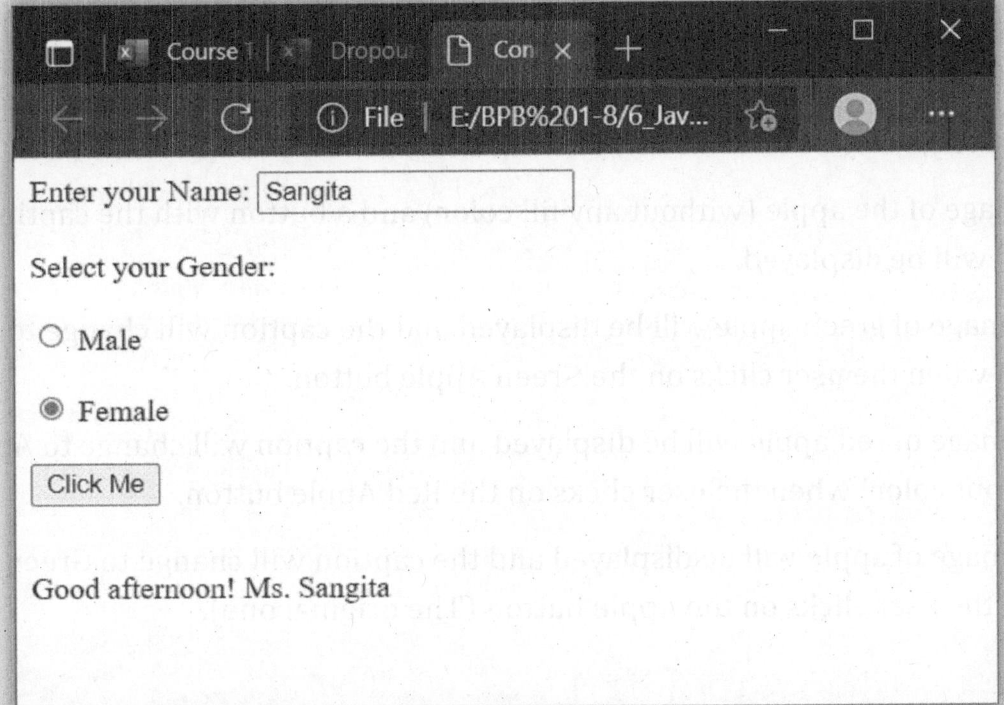

Figure 4.3(c): Output window for Activity 4.3

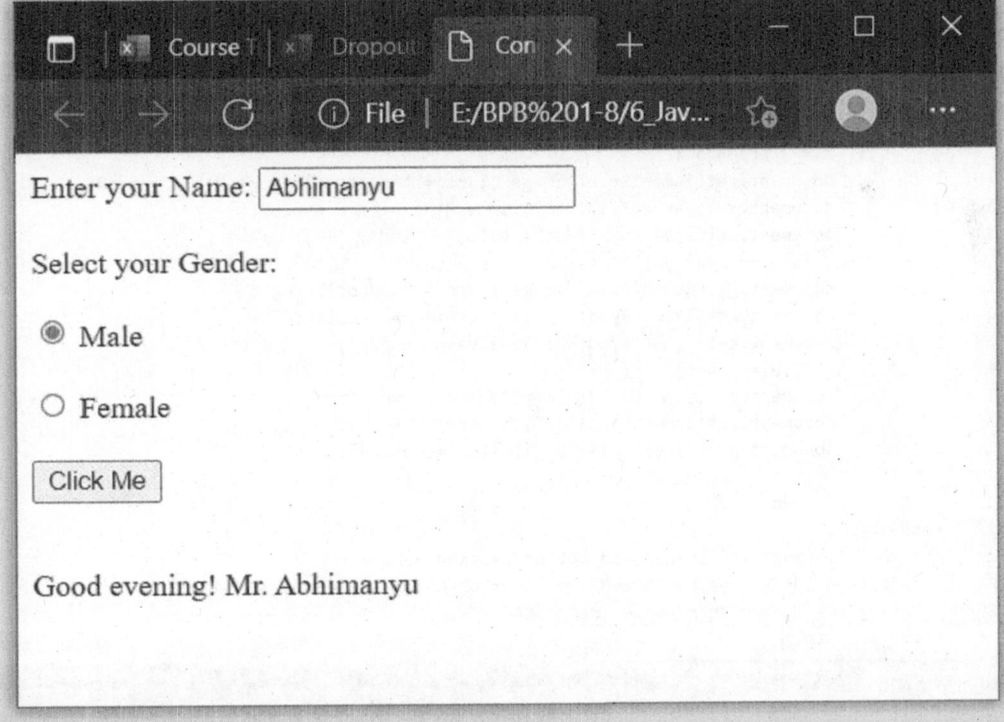

Figure 4.3(d): Output window for Activity 4.3

Activity 4.4

Toggle images and caption of the button.

In this activity,

- An image of the apple (without any fill color) and a button with the caption Green Apple will be displayed.
- The image of green apple will be displayed and the caption will change to Red Apple when the user clicks on the Green Apple button.
- The image of red apple will be displayed and the caption will change to Apple (without color) when the user clicks on the Red Apple button.
- The image of apple will be displayed and the caption will change to Green Apple when the user clicks on the Apple button (The original one).

```
<!DOCTYPE html> <html lang="en"> <head> <title>Image</title>
<style>  body { margin: 50px; }
    img { height: 200px; border: 2px solid rgb(98, 0, 255); }
</style>
<script>
    function change() {
      var a = document.getElementById('b1').value;
      if (a == 'Green') {
          document.getElementById("image").src = "greenapple.jpg";
          document.getElementById("b1").innerHTML = "Red Apple";
          document.getElementById("b1").value = "Red";    }
      else if (a == 'Red') {
          document.getElementById("image").src = "redapple.jpg";
          document.getElementById("b1").innerHTML = "Apple";
          document.getElementById("b1").value = "Apple";    }
      else if (a == 'Apple') {
          document.getElementById("image").src = "apple.jpg";
          document.getElementById("b1").innerHTML = "Green Apple";
          document.getElementById("b1").value = "Green";    }
    }
</script> </head>
<body>
    <h1> Playing with images and button caption </h1>   <br>
    <button id="b1" value="Green" onclick="change()"> Green Apple</button> <br> <br>
    <img id="image" src="apple.jpg" alt="">
</body> </html>
```

Figure 4.4(a): Code window for Activity 4.4

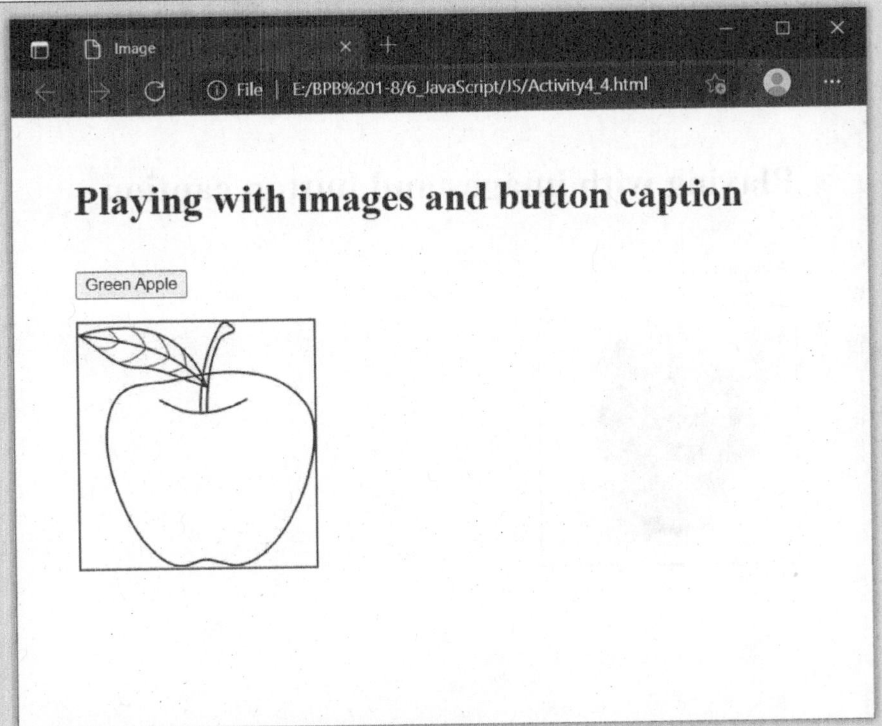

Figure 4.4(b): Output window for Activity 4.4

Figure 4.4(c): Output window for Activity 4.4

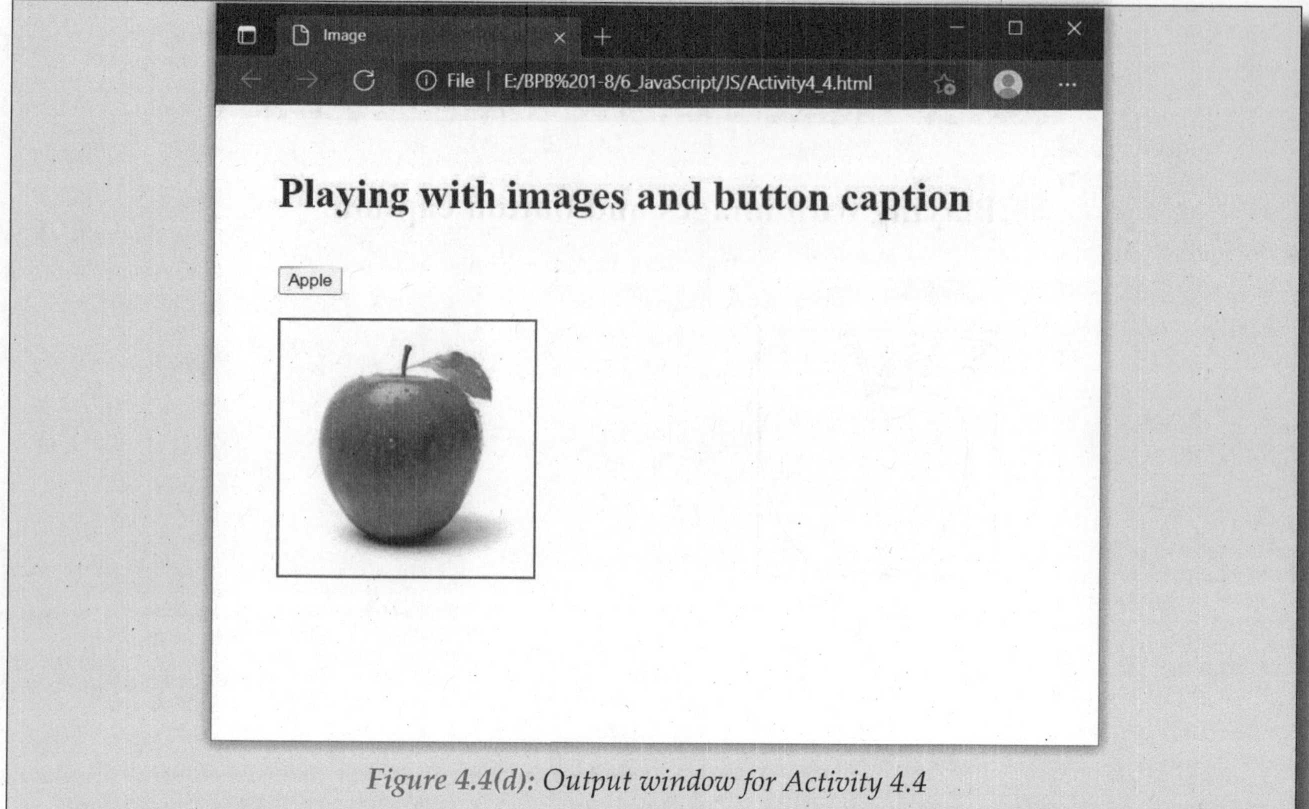

Figure 4.4(d): Output window for Activity 4.4

Clock (Version 1)

In this clock, the current system time will be displayed on the browser but will need to click on the refresh button to keep getting the updated time.

```
<!DOCTYPE html>
<html lang="en"> <head> <title>Clock</title>
<style>
    #c {
        float: right; padding: 15px;
        background-color: blanchedalmond; text-align: center;
        font-family: verdana;  font-size: 22px;  font-weight: bolder;
       }
</style>
<script>
function clock() {
    var h = new Date().getHours();
    var m = new Date().getMinutes();
    var s = new Date().getSeconds();
    if (h < 10) { h = '0' + h; /* Add 0 if hours is single digit */ }
    if (m < 10) { m = '0' + m; /* Add 0 if mins is single digit */ }
    if (s < 10) { s = '0' + s; /* Add 0 if sec is single digit */ }
    document.getElementById("c").innerHTML = h + " : " + m + " : " + s;
    }
</script>
</head>
<body onload="clock()">
    <div id="c"> </div>
</body>
</html>
```

Figure 4.5(a): Code window for Version 1 of Project Calculator

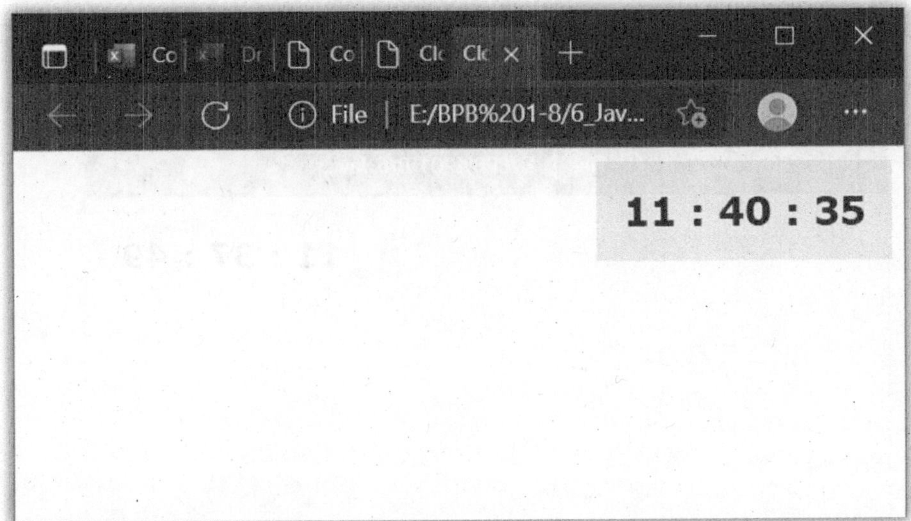

Figure 4.5(b): Output window for Version 1 of Project Calculator

Real-Time Clock (Version 2)

In this clock is created to keep changing and displaying the time on the browser without user intervention. So, now the user need not click on refreshing the webpage to display the current system time. It will be updated automatically.

```
<!DOCTYPE html>
<html lang="en"> <head> <title>Clock</title>
<style>
  #c {   float: right; padding: 15px;
         background-color: blanchedalmond; text-align: center;
         font-family: verdana; font-size: 22px; font-weight: bolder;
     }
</style>
<script>
function clock() {
    var h = new Date().getHours();
    var m = new Date().getMinutes();
    var s = new Date().getSeconds();
    if (h < 10) { h = '0' + h; /* Add 0 if hours is single digit */ }
    if (m < 10) { m = '0' + m; /* Add 0 if mins is single digit */ }
    if (s < 10) { s = '0' + s; /* Add 0 if sec is single digit */ }
    document.getElementById("c").innerHTML = h + " : " + m + " : " + s;
    ref(); }
function ref() { var r = 1000; //refresh status 1000 ms
            myt = setTimeout('clock()', r) }
</script> </head>
<body onload="ref()">
<div id="c"> </div>
</body>
</html>
```

Figure 4.6(a): Code window for Version 2 of Project Calculator

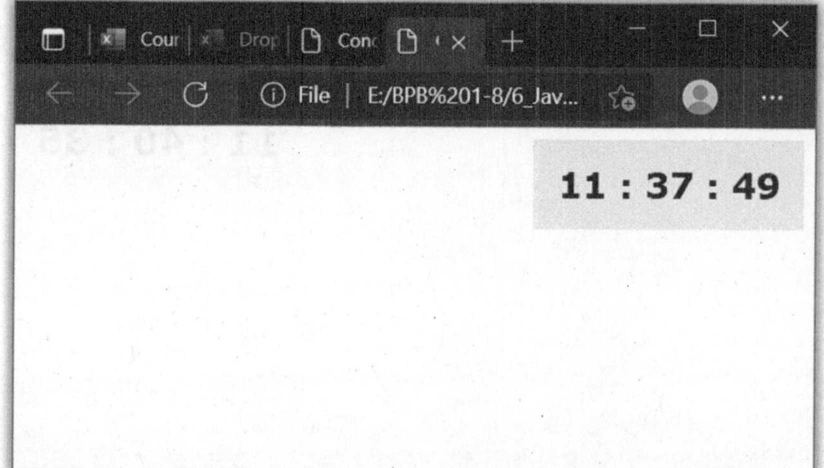

Figure 4.6(b): Output window for Version 2 of Project Calculator

Iterations and Math Object

Structure

In this chapter, you will learn and practice the following concepts:

- Looping construct
- Use of HTML elements to get the input and display a series
- Use of random method with floor method to generate random series
- Use of external style sheet to change the look of the webpage and the HTML elements of the game

Learning Objective

At the end of this chapter, you will be able to:

- Solve problems where loops are required to be used
- Display or perform some simple activity by click on some button to generate an operation that requires loop construct
- Display a list of colors in the drop-down menu randomly and choosing those colors will change the background color of the webpage
- Project –Guess the number game

Loop means repeating a set of statements multiple times in a row. Loops can also be termed as iterations.

For loop

A for loop in JavaScript is used for repeating or iterating over a sequence. That is if you wish to repeat a set of statements several times, then you can make use of a loop.

You should keep the following three things in mind while using a for loop as shown below in the example: for (a=1; a<=10; a++)

- Initial value for the variable i.e., a = 1
- Checking the condition i.e., a<=10
- Updating the value of the variablei.e., a++

Activity 5.1

Print the numbers from 1 to 10 using for loop.

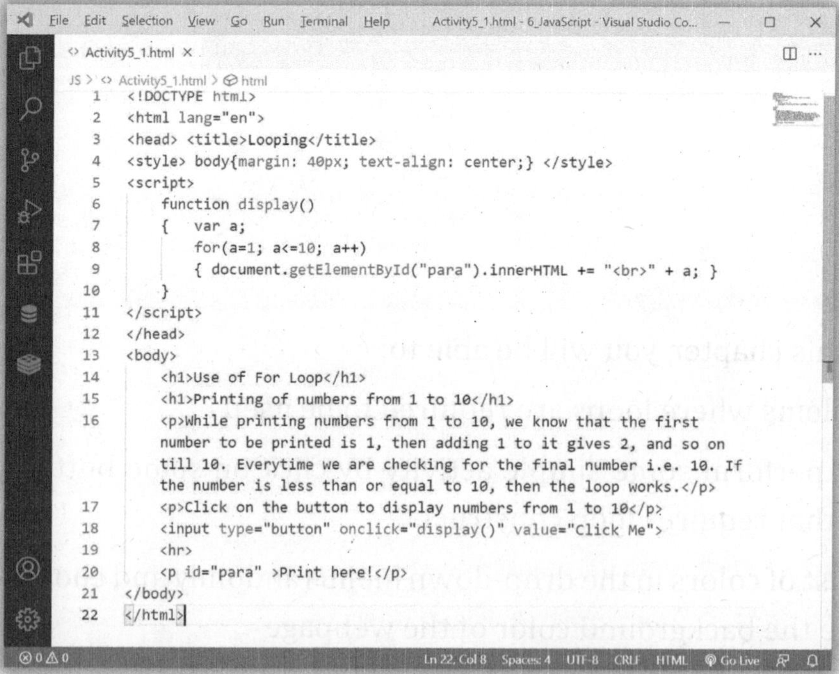

```
<!DOCTYPE html>
<html lang="en">
<head> <title>Looping</title>
<style> body{margin: 40px; text-align: center;} </style>
<script>
    function display()
    {   var a;
        for(a=1; a<=10; a++)
        { document.getElementById("para").innerHTML += "<br>" + a; }
    }
</script>
</head>
<body>
    <h1>Use of For Loop</h1>
    <h1>Printing of numbers from 1 to 10</h1>
    <p>While printing numbers from 1 to 10, we know that the first
    number to be printed is 1, then adding 1 to it gives 2, and so on
    till 10. Everytime we are checking for the final number i.e. 10. If
    the number is less than or equal to 10, then the loop works.</p>
    <p>Click on the button to display numbers from 1 to 10</p>
    <input type="button" onclick="display()" value="Click Me">
    <hr>
    <p id="para" >Print here!</p>
</body>
</html>
```

Figure 5.1(a): Code window for Activity 5.1

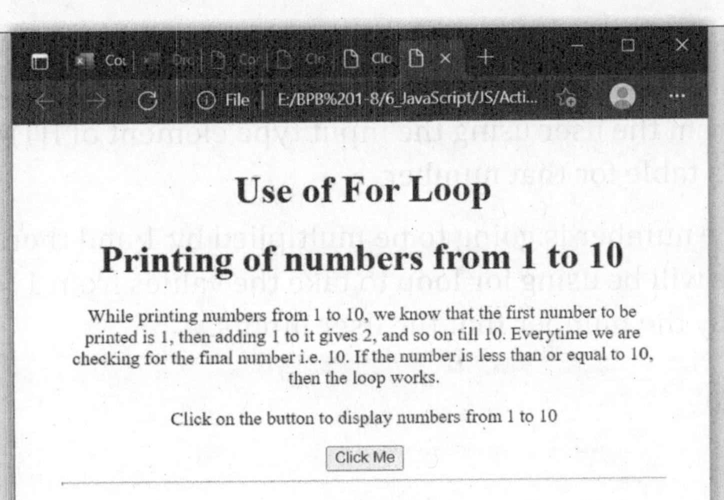

Figure 5.1(b): Output window for Activity 5.1

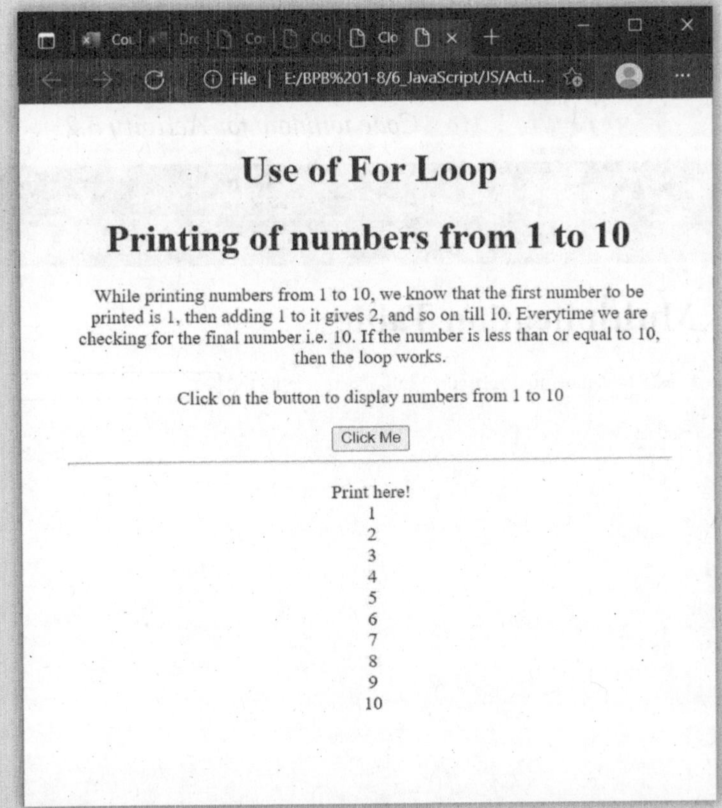

Figure 5.1(c): Output window for Activity 5.1

Activity 5.2

Read a number from the user using the input type element of HTML and then print the multiplication table for that number.

In this activity, the number is going to be multiplied by 1 and then by 2 and so on till 10. Therefore, we will be using for loop to take the values from 1 to 10 which is going to be multiplied by the number that the user inputs.

```
<!DOCTYPE html>
<html> <head> <title>Multiplication Table</title>
<script>
function func1() {
    var n = document.getElementById("tab").value;
    var s = '';
    for (var i = 1; i <= 10; i++) {
        c = n * i;
        s += n + "x" + i + "=" + c + "<br>";
    }
 document.getElementById('para').innerHTML ="Multiplication table for " + n + ": <br>"+ s;
}
</script>
</head>
<body style="margin: 20px; background-color: bisque;">
    <h1>Multiplication Table</h1>
    <label for="tab">Enter any number to display the Multiplication table for: </label>
    <input type="text" id="tab"> <br><br>
    <button id="b1" value="submit" onclick="func1()">Submit</button>
    <p id="para" style="background-color: azure; padding: 20px;"> </p>
</body>
</html>
```

Figure 5.2(a): Code window for Activity 5.2

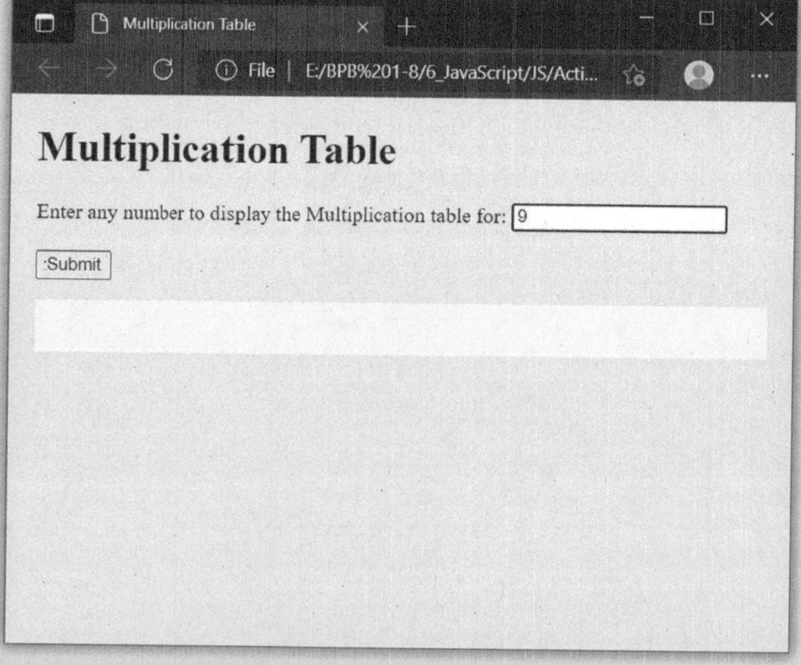

Figure 5.2(b): Output window for Activity 5.2

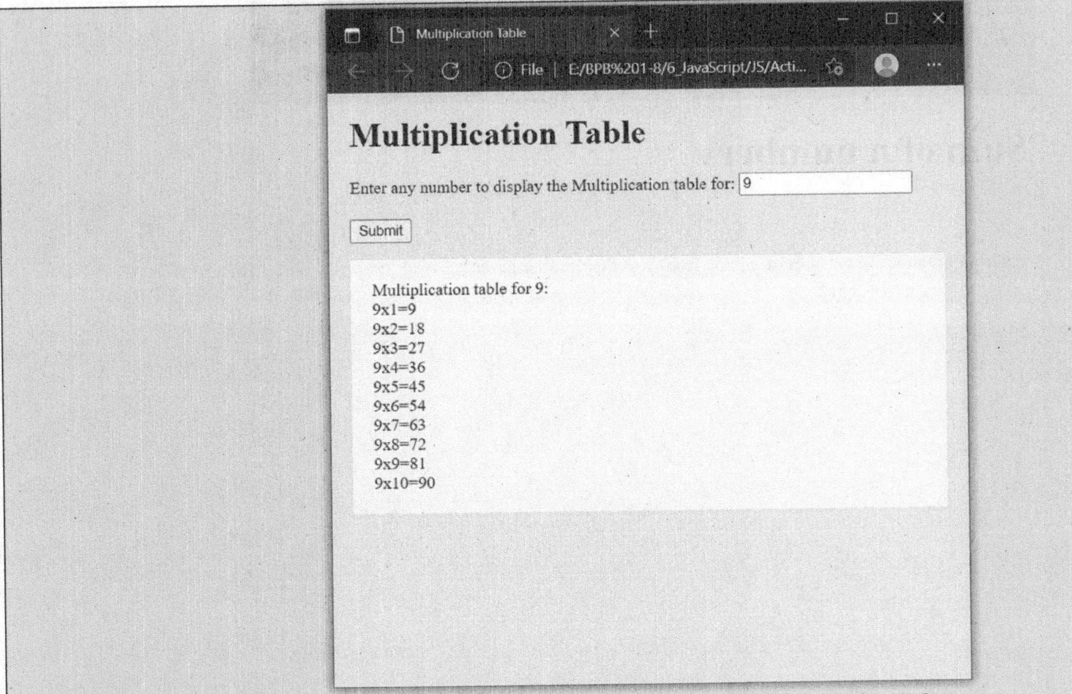

Figure 5.2(c): Output window for Activity 5.2

Activity 5.3

Print the sum of first n natural numbers after taking the nth number from the user by using the input text element of the HTML.

```
<!DOCTYPE html><html>
<head> <title>Document</title>
<script>
function func1() {
    var n = parseInt(document.getElementById("t1").value);
    var sum = 0;
    for (var i = 1; i <= n; i++) {
        sum += i;
    }
  document.getElementById("para").innerHTML="The sum of the values till " + n + " is: " + sum;
}
</script>
</head>
<body>
<h1>Sum of n numbers</h1>
<br><br>
<label for="t1"> Enter any number to get sum of all nos from 1 to the number given: </label>
<input type="text" id="t1" maxlength="20"> <br><br>
<input type="button" value="Submit" onclick="func1()">
<p id="para"> </p>
</body>
</html>
```

Figure 5.3(a): Code window for Activity 5.3

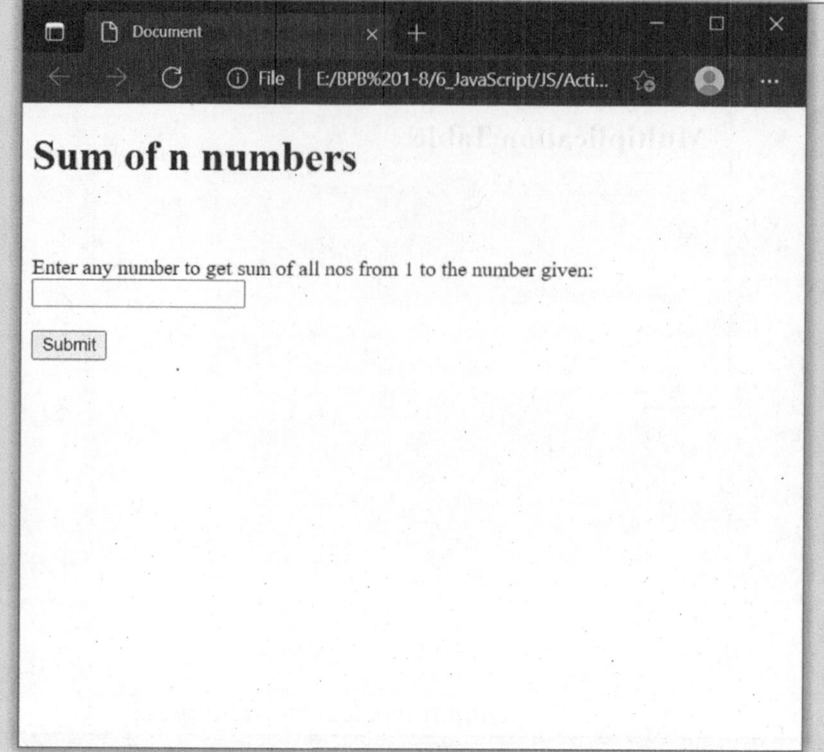

Figure 5.3(b): Output window for Activity 5.3

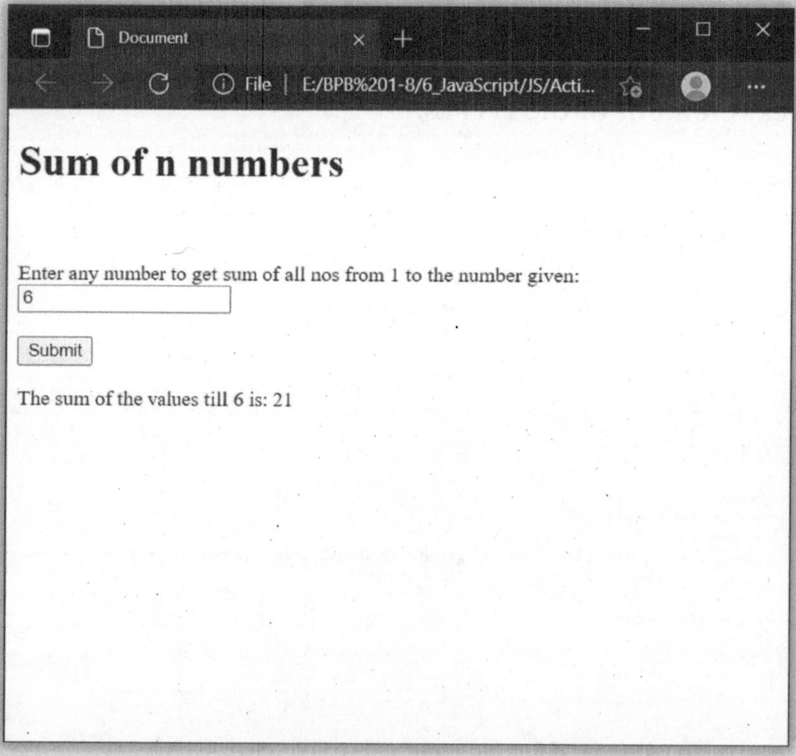

Figure 5.4(c): Output window for Activity 5.3

Activity 5.4

To read a number from the user using the input type element of HTML and then print the factors of that number.

```
<!DOCTYPE html>
<html>
<head> <title>Document</title>
<script>
  function factors() {
    var n = parseInt(document.getElementById("t1").value);
    var x = "Factors for " + n + ": ";
    var y = "";
    for (var i = 1; i <= n; i++) {
        if(n%i==0)
        { y += i + "  "; }
    }
    document.getElementById("para").innerHTML = x + y;
  }
</script>
</head>
<body>
    <h1>Factors for a number </h1>
    <br><br>
    <label for="t1"> Enter any number to display its factors: </label>
    <input type="text" id="t1" maxlength="20"> <br><br>
    <input type="button" value="Submit" onclick="factors()">
    <p id="para" style="font-weight: bolder; background-color: bisque; padding:20px"> </p>
</body>
</html>
```

Figure 5.4(a): Code window for Activity 5.4

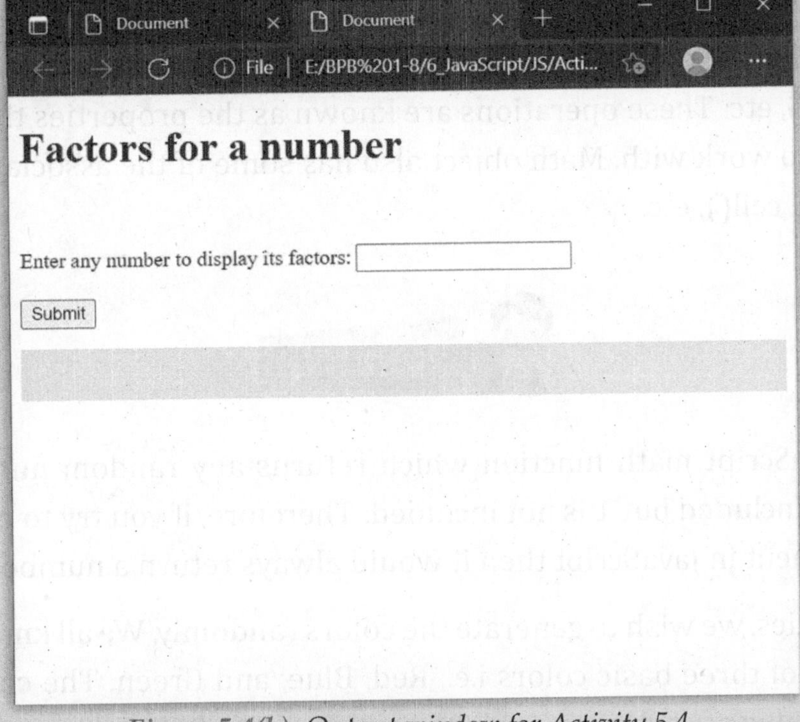

Figure 5.4(b): Output window for Activity 5.4

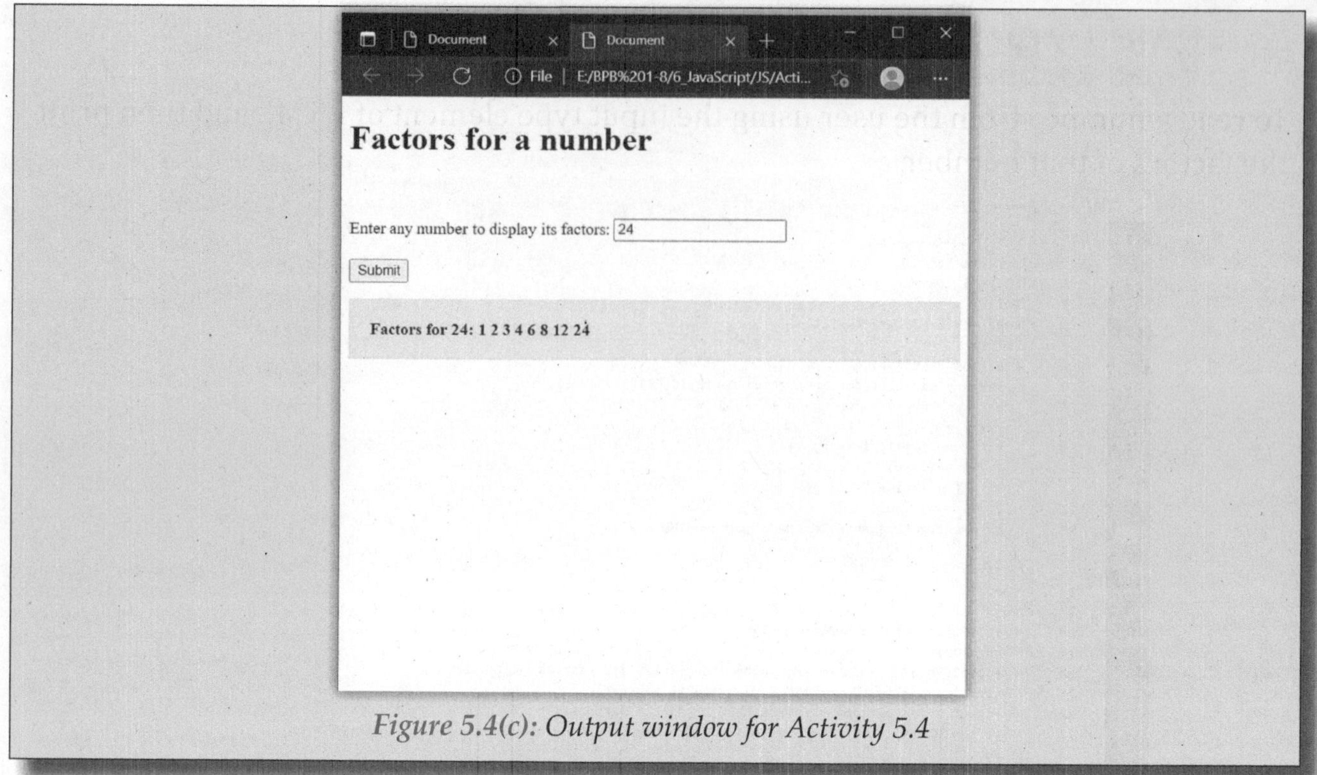

Figure 5.4(c): Output window for Activity 5.4

Math is an object in JavaScript that allows performing some of the mathematical operations like PI, SQRT, LOG, etc. These operations are known as the properties that are used with the object Math to work with. Math object also has some of the associated methods like a floor(), round(), ceil(), etc.

Random is a JavaScript math function which returns any random number between 0 and 1 where 0 is included but 1 is not included. Therefore, if you try to render the **Math. random()** statement in JavaScript then it would always return a number less than 1.

Now in our activities, we wish to generate the colors randomly. We all know that any color is a combination of three basic colors i.e., Red, Blue, and Green. The color is generated by choosing the value of each gradient in the range of 0 to 255. Now, we will be using the following statement to generate an integer between 0 to 255 to generate the different colors every time by using two functions **Math.random()** within **Math.floor()**:

Math.floor(Math.random() * 256)

Activity 5.5

To generate a random color and change the background color of the webpage using the generated color by clicking on the button.

In this activity, when the user click on the button, the background color will be changed by generating a random color and this will keep changing the background color randomly by clicking on the button.

```html
<!DOCTYPE html>
<html>
<head> <title>Random color</title>
<script>
function colorGen() {
   var r = Math.floor(Math.random() * 256);
   var g = Math.floor(Math.random() * 256);
   var b = Math.floor(Math.random() * 256);
   bgcolor1 = "rgb(" + r + ", " + g + ", " + b + ")";
   document.getElementById('color1').style.backgroundColor = bgcolor1;
}
</script>
</head>
<body id="color1">
<h1>Change the background color of the webpage using the button given below</h1>
<input type="button" id="btn1" value="Click Me!" onclick="colorGen()" style="font-weight: bold;
font-size: 20px; border: 4px solid black">
</body>
</html>
```

Figure 5.5(a): Code window for Activity 5.5

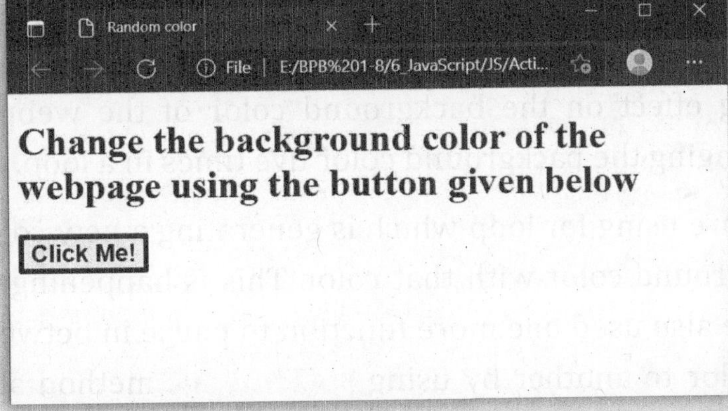

Figure 5.5(b): Output window for Activity 5.5

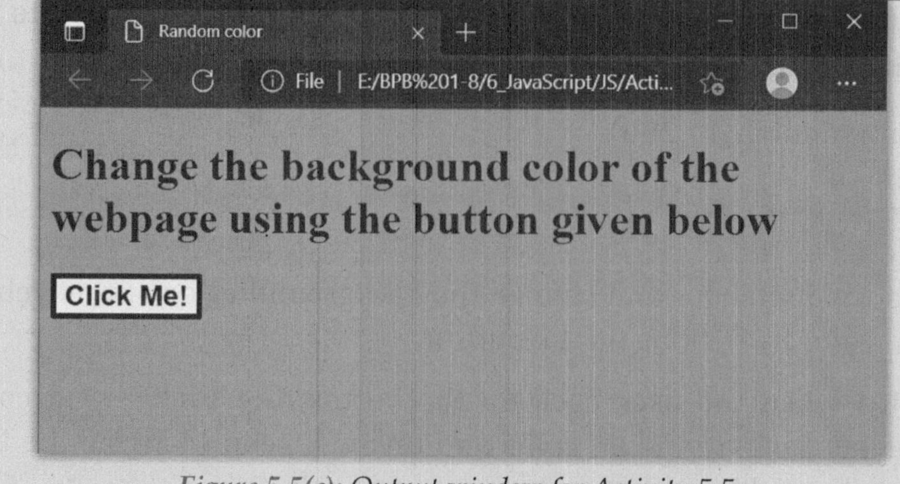

Figure 5.5(c): Output window for Activity 5.5

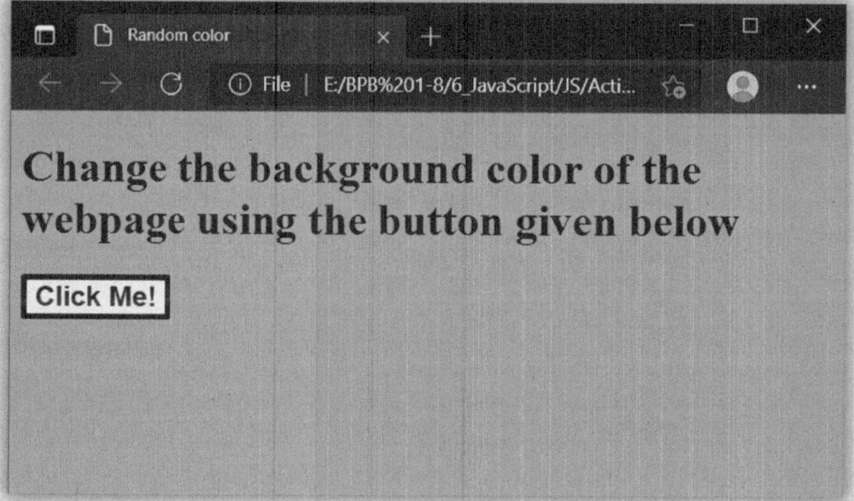

Figure 5.5(d): Output window for Activity 5.5

Activity 5.6

Create the blinking effect on the background color of the webpage by randomly generating and changing the background color five times in a loop.

In this activity, we are using for loop which is generating a new color every time and changing the background color with that color. This is happening while loading the page. Here, we have also used one more function to pause in between changing from one background color to another by using **setTimeout** method allows running the pieces of code after a certain period

```
<!DOCTYPE html> <html> <head><title>Random color</title>
<script>
function colorGen() {
 for(var a=0;a<5;a++)
  { (function(a){ window.setTimeout(function() {
    var r = Math.floor(Math.random() * 256);
    var g = Math.floor(Math.random() * 256);
    var b = Math.floor(Math.random() * 256);
    bgcolor1 = "rgb(" + r + ", " + g + ", " + b + ")";
    document.getElementById('color1').style.backgroundColor = bgcolor1;
    document.getElementById('col').innerHTML += bgcolor1 +"<br>";
    }, a*2000);
  }(a));
 }
}
</script> </head>
<body id="color1" onload="colorGen()">
<h1 id="col">Changing the Background color to  </h1>
</body>
</html>
```

Figure 5.6(a): Code window for Activity 5.6

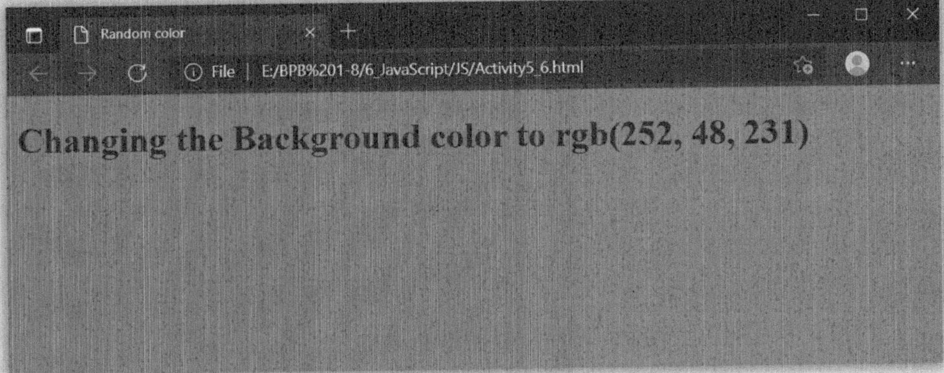

Figure 5.6(b): Output window for Activity 5.6

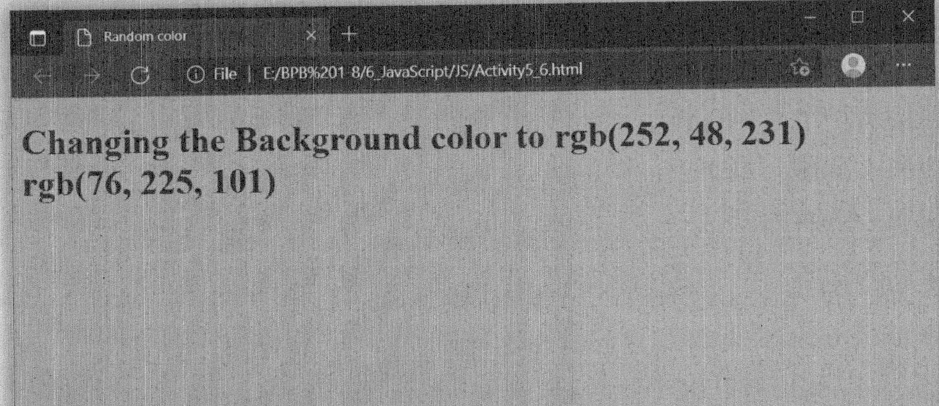

Figure 5.6(c): Output window for Activity 5.6

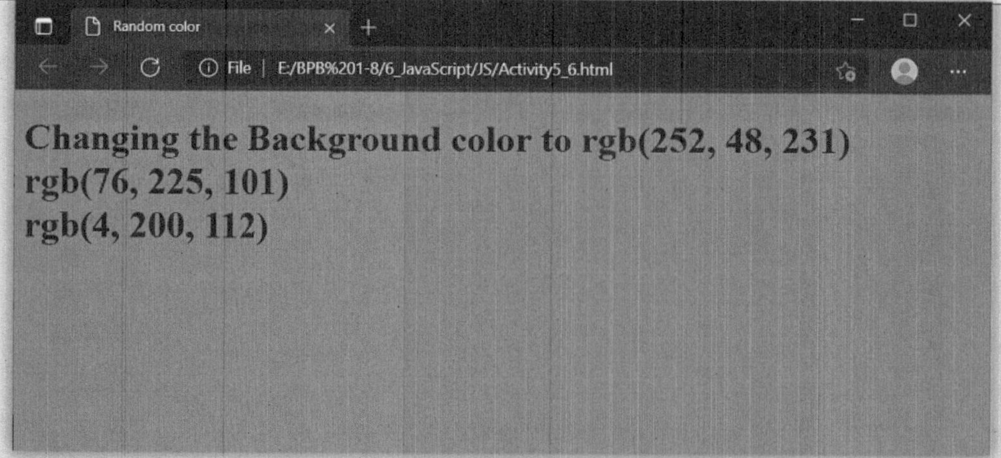

Figure 5.6(d): Output window for Activity 5.6

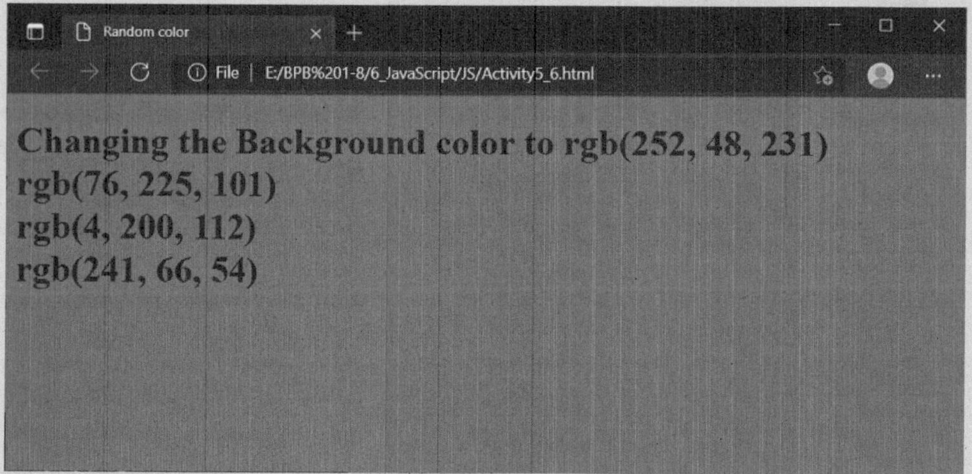

Figure 5.6(e): Output window for Activity 5.6

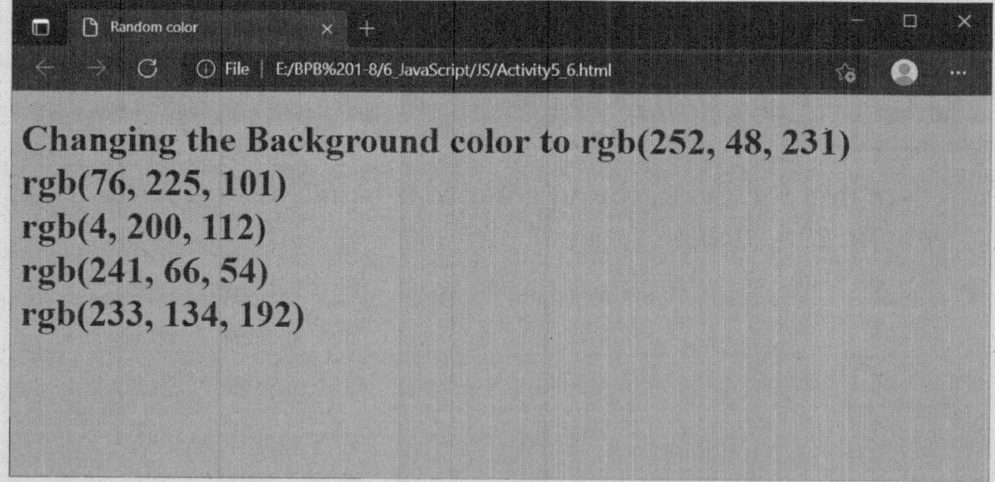

Figure 5.6(f): Output window for Activity 5.6

PROJECT

Guess the Number game

Let us build a game – Guess the number

In this game, the computer is going to generate a number.

```
<html><head> <title>Number Guessing Game</title>
<style>
body {
    font-family: 'verdana'; width: 50%;
    max-width: 800px;  min-width: 480px;
    margin: 0 auto;
    }
h1 { margin-top: 20px;  color: blue; }
</style>
</head>
<body>
<h1>Guess The Number</h1>
<p>Computer has selected the number between 1 and 10. </p>
<p>Guess the number:</p>
<label for="guessField">Enter your guess: </label>
<input type="text" id="guessField" class="guessField">
<input type="button" value="Submit guess" id="submitguess">
<script>
 var y = Math.floor(Math.random() * 10 + 1); // random value is stored in y
 var guess = 1; // counter guess to check no of guesses
// this function will keep working till the correct guess matches with
    the number generated
 // The function will be called till the time user guess matches with the number
 document.getElementById("submitguess").onclick = function ()
  {
    // number guessed by user
    var x = document.getElementById("guessField").value;
```

```
    if (x == y) {
            alert("CONGRATULATIONS!!! YOU GUESSED IT RIGHT IN "
                + guess + " GUESS ");
             }
    else if (x > y) /* if guessed number is greater than actual number*/
         {
             guess++;
             alert("OOPS SORRY!! TRY A SMALLER NUMBER");
           }
    else { /* if guessed number is smaller than actual number*/
            guess++;
            alert("OOPS SORRY!! TRY A GREATER NUMBER")
           }
  }
</script></body></html>
```

Figure 5.7(a): Code window for Project – Guess the number

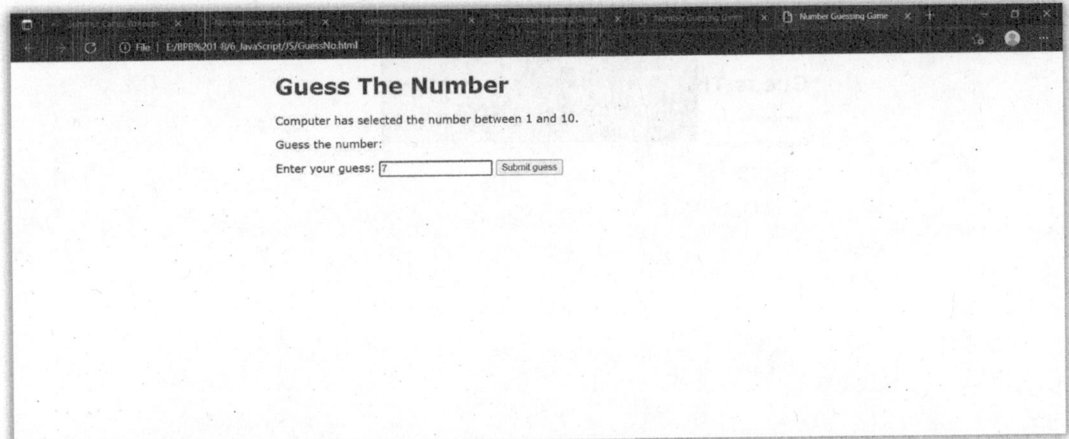

Figure 5.7(b): Output window for Project – Guess the number

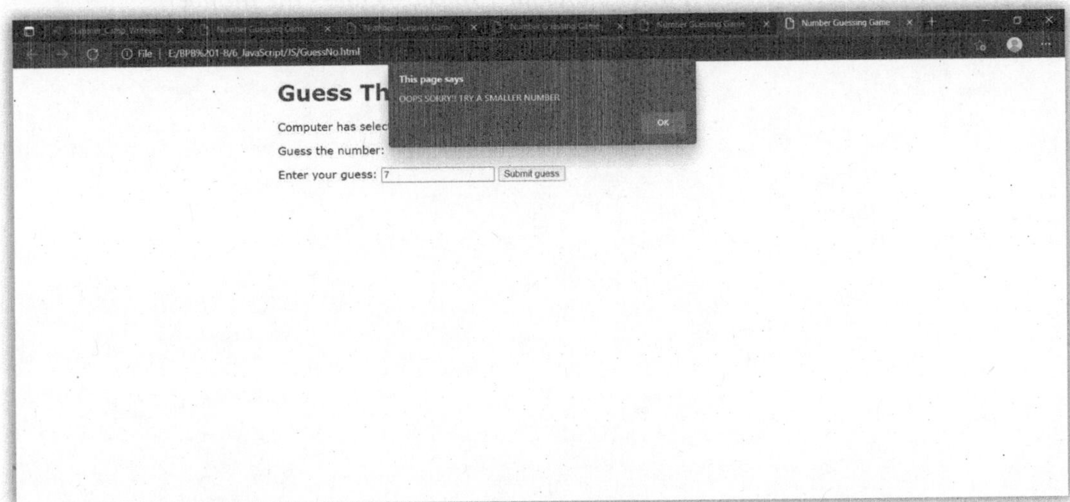

Figure 5.7(c): Output window for Project – Guess the number

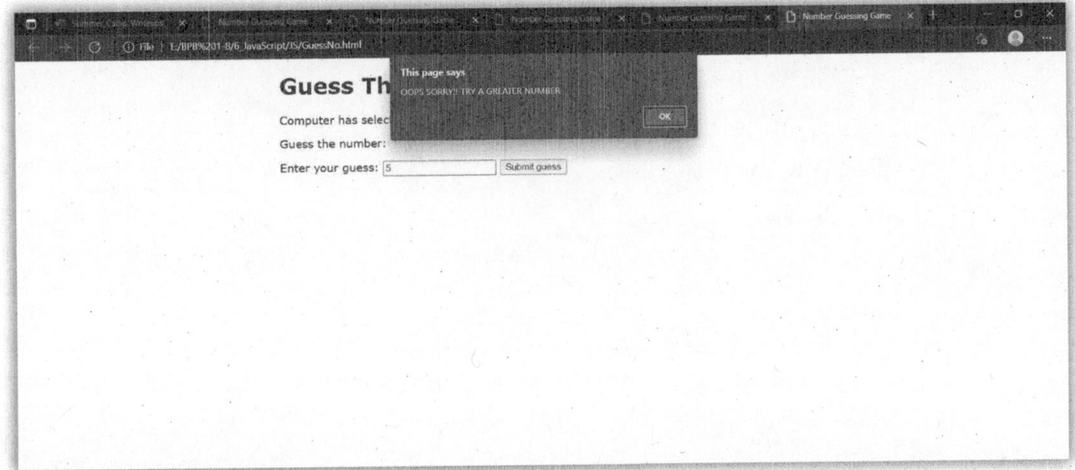

Figure 5.7(d): Output window for Project – Guess the number

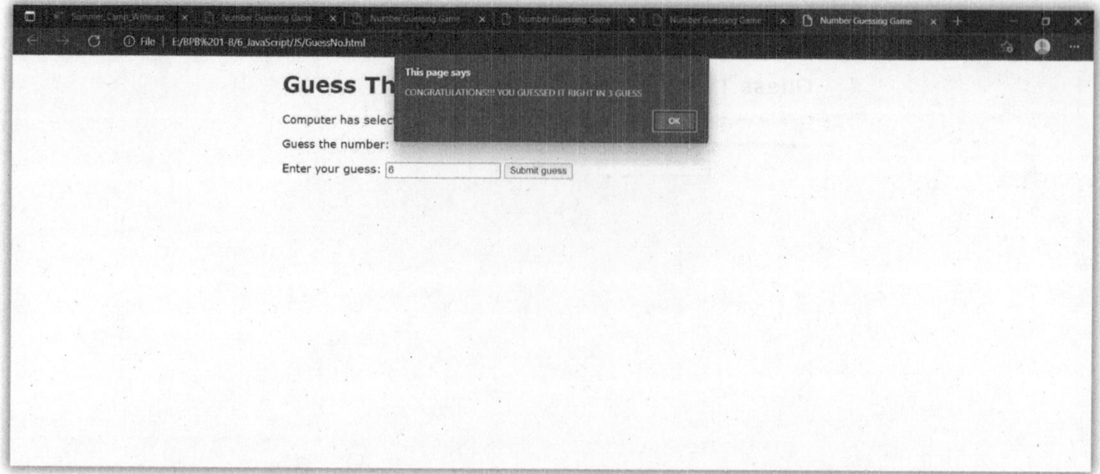

Figure 5.7(e): Output window for Project – Guess the number

HTML Canvas and Animation

Structure

In this chapter, you will learn and practice the following concepts:

- Creating a canvas
- Drawing different shapes
- Filling the shapes with colors
- Animating the images using HTML and CSS
- Making Greeting Card using images and drawing objects

Learning Objective

At the end of this chapter, you will be able to:

- Any type of drawing objects for the webpage
- Create a motion feature in the object to animate
- Project –Greeting Card

Canvas

It is an HTML element that acts as a drawing surface that one can use to draw 2d shapes using JavaScript.

Info bot

The default size of the canvas is 300 pixels (width) x 150 pixels (height).

The basic steps to be followed while making use of canvas as a drawing surface using JavaScript are:

Step 1: Create an object to represent the <canvas> element by **document.getElementById()** method.

Step 2: Create another object/ variable which will act as a pen tool to draw on the canvas by using the **getContext()** method.

Activity 6.1

To draw the canvas on the webpage which will be displayed by using the style properties of the internal style sheet.

```
File Edit Selection View Go Run Terminal Help    Activity6_1.html - 6_JavaScript - Visual Studio Code
Activity6_1.html ×
JS > Activity6_1.html > html
<!DOCTYPE html>
<html lang="en">
<head>
<title>Canvas</title>
</head>
<body>
<canvas style="width: 600px; height: 600px; border: 2px solid black;">
</canvas>
</body>
</html>
Ln 10, Col 8  Spaces: 4  UTF-8  CRLF  HTML  Go Live
```

Figure 6.1(a): Code window for Activity 6.1

Activity 6.2

To draw the canvas on the webpage which will be shown by calling the JavaScript function **disp()** on the load event of the body tag.

```
<!DOCTYPE html>
<html lang="en">
<head><title>Canvas</title>
<script>
function disp()
 {
    var c = document.getElementById('can');
    var pen = c.getContext('2d');
    // Set the background color for the canvas
    c.style.backgroundColor = 'rgba(0,120,200,10)';
    c.style.width = "600px"; //Set the width of the canvas
    c.style.height = "600px"; //Set the height of the canvas
 }
</script>
</head>
<body onload="disp()">
    <canvas id="can"></canvas>
</body>
</html>
```

Figure 6.2(a): Code window for Activity 6.2

Figure 6.2(b): Code window for Activity 6.2

Activity 6.3

To draw two rectangles, one rectangle by filling the color and the other one without filling the color.

Info bot

The coordinate of canvas for top, left is 0, 0.

- **fillStyle** is used to choose the color for the rectangle to be filled.
- **fillRect** is used to create a rectangle with x, y, width, height coordinates and will fill the rectangle using the color which is mentioned using the fill Style property.
- **strokeStyle** is used to choose the border color for the object to be drawn.
- **strokeRect** is used to draw a rectangle with x, y, width, height coordinates with the border color which is mentioned using the stroke Style property.

```
<!DOCTYPE html>
<html lang="en">
<head> <title>Canvas</title>
<script>
 function disp() {
    var c = document.getElementById('can');
    var pen = c.getContext('2d');
    c.style.width = "600px";
    c.style.height = "600px";
    c.style.border = "2px solid black";
    c.style.backgroundColor = 'rgba(230,220,250)';
    // A rectangle with border
    pen.strokeStyle='black';
    pen.strokeRect(12, 12, 50, 60);
    // A rectange with filled colored rectangle
    pen.fillStyle = 'pink';
    pen.fillRect(80, 50, 40, 30);
}
</script>
</head>
<body onload="disp()">
<h1>Drawing Rectangle</h1>
<p>Let us draw two rectangles of different sizes at different coordinates. </p>
<canvas id="can"></canvas>
</body>
</html>
```

Figure 6.3(a): Code window for Activity 6.3

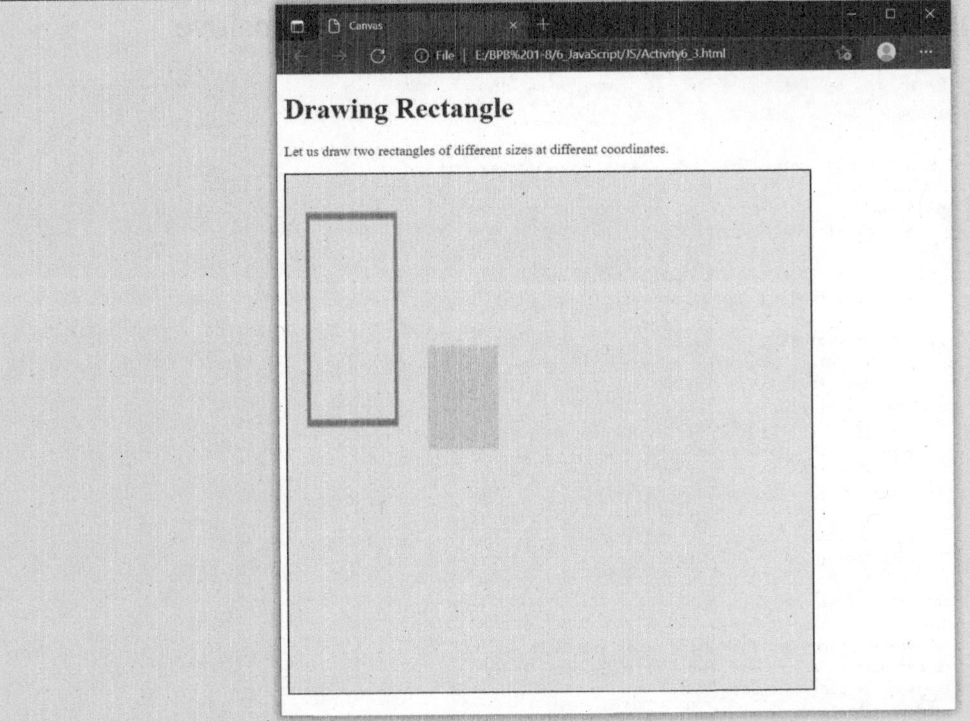

Figure 6.3(b): Output window for Activity 6.3

Activity 6.4

To draw a line and a triangle using lines.

To draw a line on the canvas, we require the following commands in JavaScript:

- **moveTo(x, y)** that defines starting coordinates of the line.
- **lineTo(x, y)** that defines the ending coordinates of the line.
- **stroke()** needs to be invoked to draw the line specified by the moveTo coordinates to lineTo coordinates.

So, to draw the triangle, we require three lines. For each line to be drawn, we require one set of the following commands:

- moveTo()
- lineTo()
- stroke()

Info bot

JavaScript is a case-sensitive language.

Note: Remember to type in the commands properly as it is case-sensitive.

```
<!DOCTYPE html> <html lang="en"> <head> <title>Canvas</title>
<script>
function disp() {
    var c = document.getElementById('can');
    var pen = c.getContext('2d');
    c.style.width = "600px"; c.style.height = "600px";
    c.style.border = "10px solid red";
    c.style.backgroundColor = 'rgba(230,220,250)';
    pen.lineWidth='2';
    pen.moveTo(20, 20); //Defines the starting x,y
    pen.lineTo(100, 20); //Defines the ending x,y
    pen.stroke();
    // A triangle
    pen.moveTo(50, 80); pen.lineTo(200,80);
    pen.stroke();
    pen.moveTo(50,80);  pen.lineTo(125,40);
    pen.stroke();
    pen.moveTo(125,40); pen.lineTo(200,80);
    pen.stroke();
}
</script> </head>
<body onload="disp()">
<h1>Drawing Lines and then using lines a triagle </h1>
<p>Let us draw a line and then a triangle using lines. </p>
<canvas id="can"></canvas>
</body> </html>
```

Figure 6.4(a): Code window for Activity 6.4

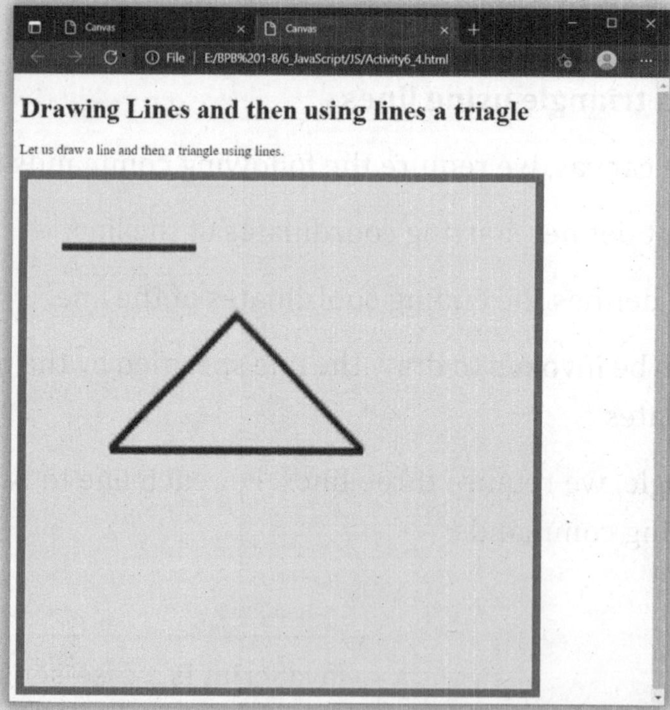

Figure 6.4(b): Output window for Activity 6.4

Activity 6.5

Draw arcs and circle using JavaScript commands in the canvas.

```
<!DOCTYPE html>
<html lang=”en”>
<head><title>Canvas</title>
<script>
function disp() {
     var c = document.getElementById(‘can’);
     var pen = c.getContext(‘2d’);
     c.style.width = “600px”; c.style.height = “600px”;
     c.style.border = “10px solid red”;
     c.style.backgroundColor = ‘rgba(230,250,250)’;
     pen.lineWidth=’2’;
     // 1/4th arc
     pen.arc(40, 30, 20, 0, 0.5*Math.PI);
     pen.stroke();
     pen.moveTo(90,30);
     // 1/2 arc
     pen.arc(90, 30, 20, 0, 1 * Math.PI);
     pen.stroke();
     pen.moveTo(150,30);
     pen.arc(150,30, 20, 0, 1.5*Math.PI);
     pen.stroke();
     pen.beginPath();
     pen.moveTo(200, 30);
     pen.arc(200, 30, 20, 0, 2 * Math.PI);
     pen.fillStyle = ‘pink’;
     pen.fill();
     pen.stroke();
}
</script>
</head>
<body onload=”disp()”>
<h1>Drawing Circle and different arcs </h1>
<p>Let us draw a Circle and then different arcs. </p>
```

```
<canvas id="can"></canvas>
</body>
</html>
```

Figure 6.5(a): Code window for Activity 6.5

To draw an arc, we require the following:

- **beginPath()** is used to start the path for an arc or circle.
- **arc**(x, y, radius, starting angle, ending angle) to draw an arc or circle depending upon the ending angle.
- **stroke()** needs to be invoked to draw the arc with the properties specified in the arc().The ending angle specifies the kind of arc to be drawn

The first arc drawn is with the help of starting angle as 0 and ending angle as 0.5*Math. PI, an arc will be semicircle when the ending angle is 1*Math.PI and so on.

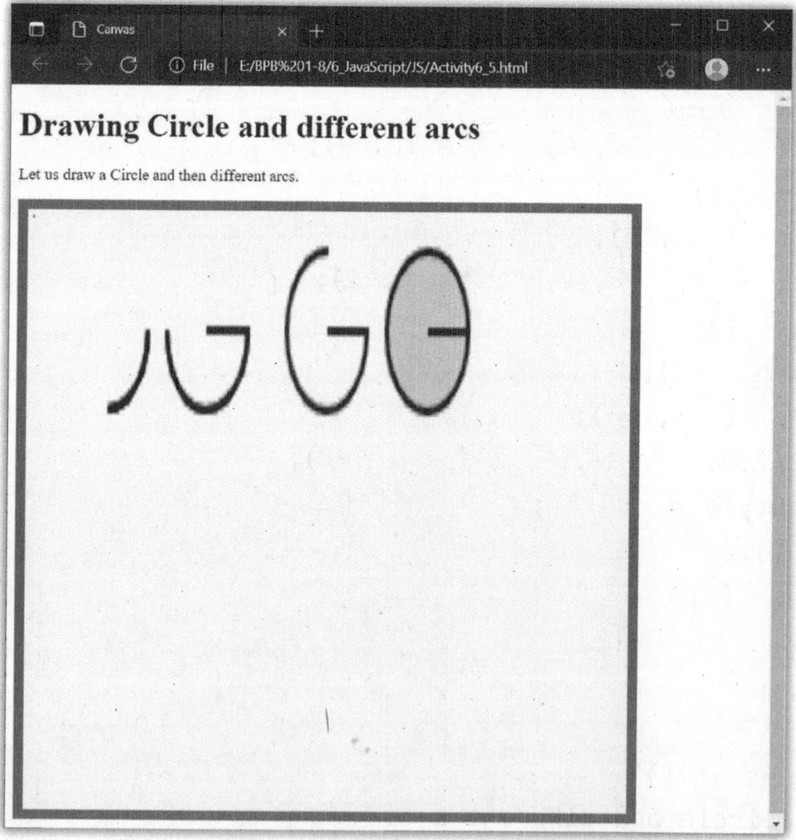

Figure 6.5(b): Output window for Activity 6.5

Activity 6.6

To draw an emoji using arcs in JavaScript on canvas.

To fill the circle, write the fillStyle command to choose the color with which the arc needs to be filled with and then call the **fill()** method and then **stroke()**.

```
<!DOCTYPE html><html lang="en"><head><title>Canvas</title>
<script>
function disp() {
    var c = document.getElementById('can');
    var pen = c.getContext('2d');
    c.style.width = "600px"; c.style.height = "600px";
    c.style.border = "10px solid red";
    c.style.backgroundColor = 'rgba(230,250,250)';
    pen.lineWidth = '2';
    pen.beginPath();
    pen.moveTo(200, 50);
    pen.arc(200, 50, 40, 0, 2 * Math.PI);
    pen.fillStyle='pink';
    pen.fill();
    pen.stroke();
    pen.moveTo(210,30);
    pen.arc(210, 33, 3, 0, 2*Math.PI);
    pen.stroke();
}
</script></head>
<body onload="disp()">
    <h1>Drawing Circle and different arcs </h1>
    <p>To draw a shape of a face </p>
    <canvas id="can"></canvas>
</body></html>
```

Activity 6.7

To draw a smiley

Figure 6.7(a): Code window for Activity 6.7

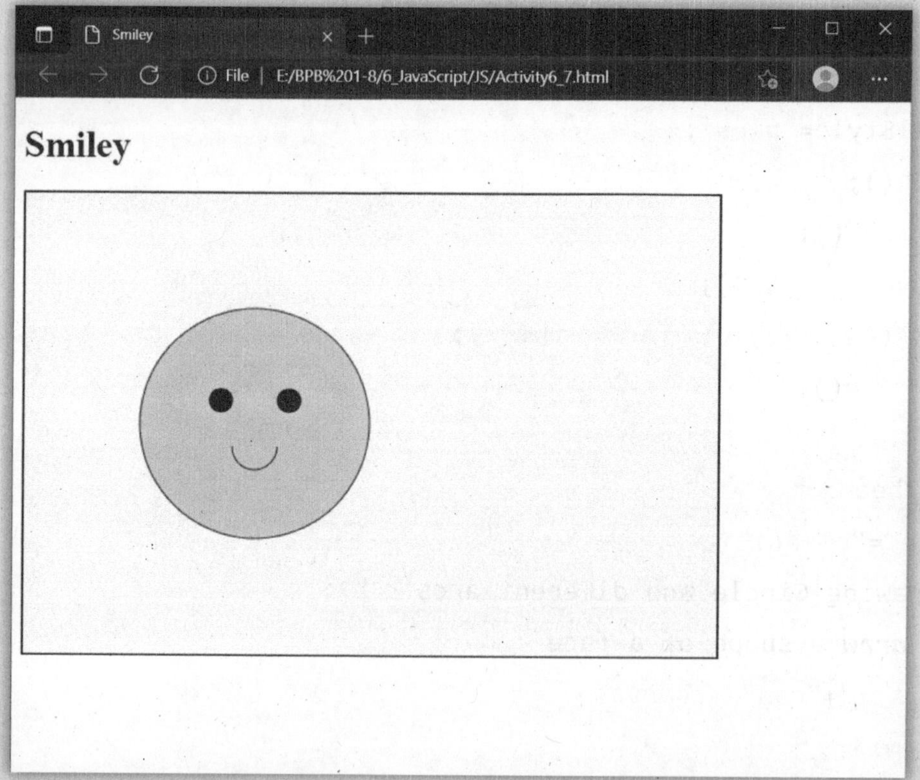

Figure 6.7(b): Output window for Activity 6.7

Activity 6.8

To write text on the canvas using JavaScript.

- fillStyle is used to choose the pen color for writing.
- textAlign to choose the alignment for the text in the canvas.
- font to choose the size and style for the text.
- fillText(string, x, y) is used to print the string in the required x and y coordinates.
- canvas.width and canvas.height is used to take the width and height of the canvas.

```html
<!DOCTYPE html>
<html lang="en">
<head><title>Text</title>
</head>
<script>
function display() {
    var canva = document.getElementById("can");
    var b = canva.getContext("2d");
    b.beginPath();
    b.fillStyle='red';
    b.textAlign='center';
    b.font='30px Jokerman';
    b.fillText("Welcome to the world of Web Programming",canva.width/2, canva.height/2-70);
}
</script>
<body onload="display()">
<h1>Display text</h1>
<canvas id="can" height="400" width="800"
        style="border: 6px solid black; background-color: rgb(226, 184, 133);"></canvas>
</body>
</html>
```

Figure 6.8(a): Code window for Activity 6.8

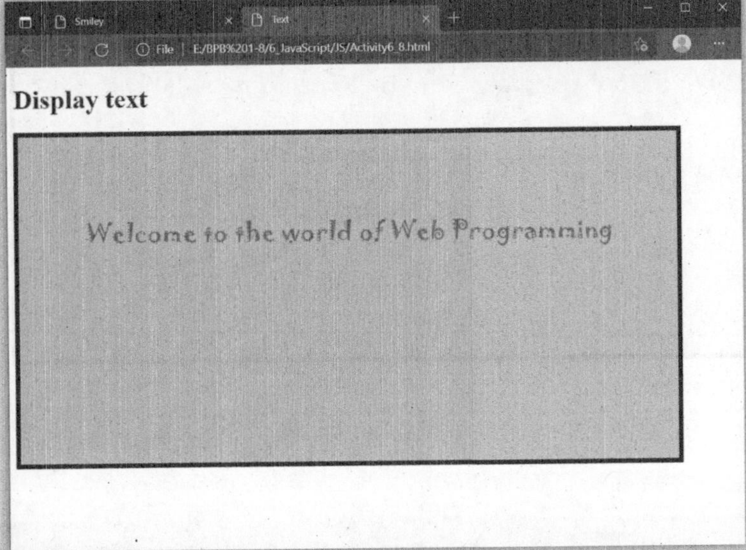

Figure 6.8(b): Output window for Activity 6.8

Activity 6.9

To display the text on the canvas using different formatting options.

```
<!DOCTYPE html> <html lang="en">
<head> <title>Text</title> </head>
<script>
function display() {
  var canva = document.getElementById("can");
  var b = canva.getContext("2d");
  b.beginPath();
  b.fillStyle = 'red';
  b.textAlign = 'center';
  b.font = '30px Jokerman';
  b.fillText("Welcome to the world of Web Programming", canva.width/2, canva.height/2 - 70);
  b.font = '40px Jokerman';
  b.strokeText("HTML, CSS & ", canva.width/2, canva.height/2);
  b.shadowOffsetX = 4;
  b.shadowOffsetY = 2;
  b.shadowBlur = 4;
  b.shadowColor = 'green';
  b.fillText('JavaScript', canva.width/2, canva.height/2 + 70);
}
</script>
<body onload="display()">
<h1>Display text in different formats</h1>
<canvas id="can" height="400" width="800"
        style="border: 6px solid black; background-color: rgb(221, 190, 218);"></canvas>
</body>
</html>
```

Figure 6.9(a): Code window for Activity 6.9

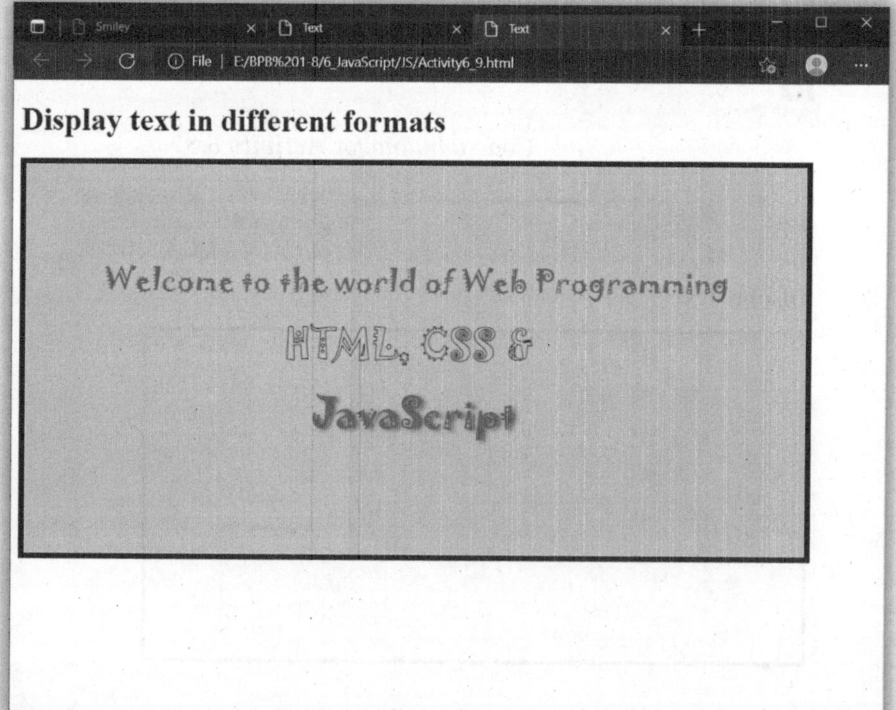

Figure 6.9(b): Output window for Activity 6.9

Cascading style sheet allows animation without using JavaScript or Flash. The animation gradually changes from the current style to the new style at a certain time frame while specifying it within the **@keyframes**.

To display four images one after the other in the form of a slide show.

Figure 6.10(a): Output window for Activity 6.10

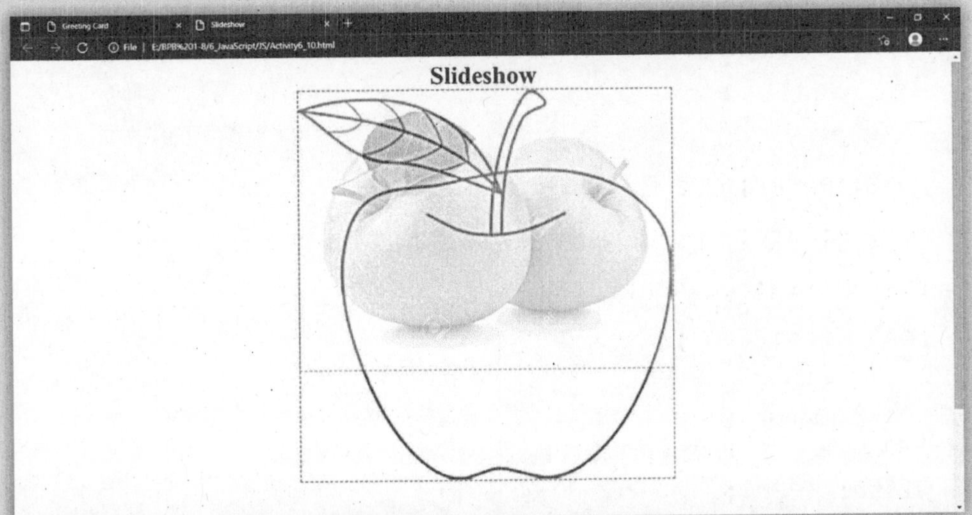

Figure 6.10(b): Output window for Activity 6.10

Figure 6.10(c): Output window for Activity 6.10

Figure 6.10(d): Output window for Activity 6.10

```
<!DOCTYPE html><html lang="en"><head><title>Slideshow</title>
<style>
    h1{
        float:center;
        margin:auto;
        text-align: center;
        font-size: 40px;
    }
    .slides{
        width: 600px;
        height: 600px;
```

```
        overflow: hidden;
        float: center;
        margin: auto;
    }
    .slides img{
        position: absolute;
        animation: slides 20s infinite;
        opacity: 0;
        width: 600px;
        height: auto;
        border: 2px dashed red;
    }
    @keyframes slides{
        25% {opacity: 1;}
        45% {opacity: 0;}
    }
    .slides img:nth-child(1) {animation-delay: 0s;}
    .slides img:nth-child(2) {animation-delay: 5s;}
    .slides img:nth-child(3) {animation-delay: 10s;}
    .slides img:nth-child(4) {animation-delay: 15s;}
</style></head>
<body><h1>Slideshow</h1>
<div class="slides">
    <img src="apple.jpg" alt="image 1">
    <img src="greenapple.jpg" alt="image 2">
    <img src="redapple.jpg" alt="image 3">
    <img src="christmas.jpg" alt="image 4">
</div></body></html>
```

Figure 6.10(e): Code window for Activity 6.10

Activity 6.11

To display the text while the cursor moves over it using the hover effect in CSS.

```
<!DOCTYPE html> <html lang="en">
<head> <title>Surprise message</title>
<style>
p{display: none;
    color: blue;
    font-family: Jokerman;
    font-size: 150%;
    background-color: peachpuff;
    padding: 20px;
}
h1{font-size: 250%;
    text-align: center;
}
div{font-family: sans-serif;
    font-size: 250%;
    color: blue;
}
div:hover p{display: block;}
a.one:hover{color: hotpink;}
a.two:hover{color:purple; font-size: 120%;}
a.three:hover{color: aqua; font-size: 200%;}
</style>
</head>
<body><h1>
        <a class="one">Surprise</a> <br>
        <a class="two">Surprise!</a> <br>
        <a class="three">Surprise!!</a> <br>
</h1>
<div>Hey!!! You have a surprise 🔒 🔒 locked here 📩 <br>
    Hover over me to 🔑 unlock the gift 🎁
<p>Tada!! <br>
Hey!! You mean so much to me... <br> This is your special day... <br>
Happy Birthday 🎊🎉🍫🎂🎊🎉
</p>
</div>
</body></html>
```

Figure 6.11(a): Code window for Activity 6.11

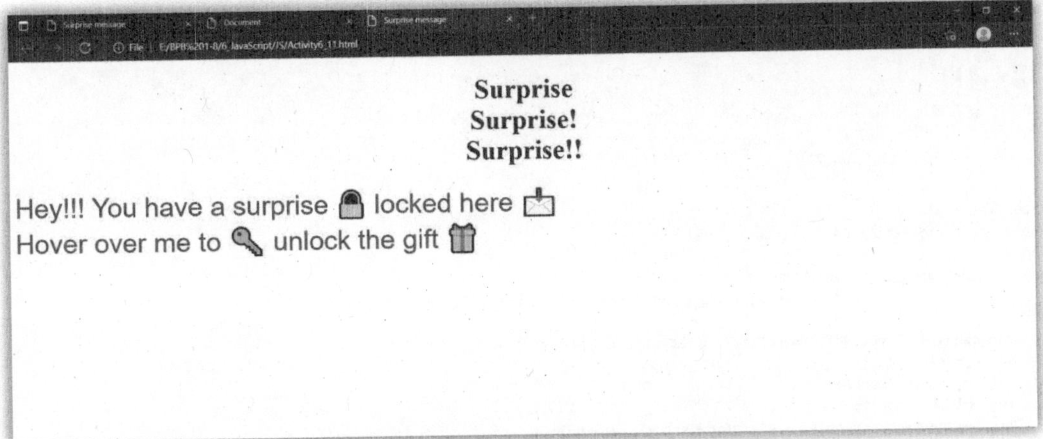

Figure 6.11(b): Output window for Activity 6.11

Figure 6.11(c): Output window for Activity 6.11

Figure 6.11(d): Output window for Activity 6.11

ROJECT

Greeting Card

```html
<!DOCTYPE html>
<head> <title>Greeting Card</title> </head>
<body>
<canvas id='canvas1' height="500" width="900"
        style="border-radius: 40px; background-image: url(snowacutal.jpeg);"></canvas>
<script>
    var can = document.getElementById('canvas1');
    var b = can.getContext('2d');
    var img = new Image();
    img.onload = start;
    img.onerror = function () { alert(img.src + 'failed'); }
    img.src = "christmastree.png";
    function start() {
        b.drawImage(img, 90, 90, 300, 300);
    }
    b.fillStyle = "white";
    b.font = "90px 'orange juice'";
    b.fillText("   Merry   ", 500, 200);
    b.fillText("Christmas!", 500, 280);
    b.arc(240, 240, 200, 0, 360);
    b.stroke();
    b.fillStyle = "white";
    b.stroke();
    b.fill();
</script>
</body> </html>
```

Figure 6.12(a): Code window for the project- Greeting Card

Figure 6.12(b): Output window for the project- Greeting Card